Better Homes and Gardens.

ENCYCLOPEDIA
of
COOKING

Volume 7

A favorite home-baked dessert features Basic Apple Dumplings. Each juicy apple, tucked inside a pastry shell, is basted
with maple syrup during baking. (See *Dumplings* for recipe.)

On the cover: Whether the doughnuts are shaped in the familiar rings, cut in squares, twisted, or filled with fruit they are
always delicious at snacktime and for coffeebreaks.

BETTER HOMES AND GARDENS BOOKS
NEW YORK • DES MOINES

©Meredith Corporation, 1970, 1971, 1973. All Rights Reserved.
Printed in the United States of America.
Special Edition. Second Printing, 1974.
Library of Congress Catalog Card Number: 73-83173
SBN: 696-02027-0

DEVILED — 1. A broiled version of poultry. 2. A highly seasoned mixture that is most generally finely chopped.

When deviled refers to the way in which poultry is cooked, the recipe usually includes the title *à la Diable*. To prepare poultry in this manner, the bird is slit down the back, spread flat, and pounded. The exposed surfaces are brushed with butter or oil, seasoned, and then the bird is broiled. Just before the end of the cooking period, soft bread crumbs are liberally sprinkled over the bird. Broiling continues until the topping is browned.

The more familiar usage of deviled implies a highly seasoned food. A zippy flavor is achieved by the use of hot seasonings, such as black and cayenne pepper, hot pepper sauce, Worcestershire sauce, mustard, horseradish, or garlic. Classic Deviled Eggs is probably the best-known recipe illustrating this term.

Classic Deviled Eggs

      6 hard-cooked eggs, halved
         lengthwise
    ¼ cup mayonnaise or salad
         dressing
      1 tablespoon finely chopped onion
      1 tablespoon finely chopped
         pimiento-stuffed green
         olives (optional)
    1½ teaspoons prepared mustard

Remove egg yolks from whites. Mash yolks; blend with mayonnaise, onion, olives, mustard, ⅛ teaspoon salt, and dash pepper. Refill whites, using pastry tube, if desired. Chill. Garnish with paprika, if desired. Makes 12.

Baked Deviled Tomatoes

Place 8 large tomato halves, cut side up, in baking dish. Sprinkle with a little salt. Spread tops with 1 tablespoon prepared mustard. Combine 2 tablespoons chopped green pepper; 2 tablespoons chopped celery; 1 tablespoon chopped green onion; and 2 tablespoons butter or margarine, melted. Spoon over tomatoes. Bake at 425° for 8 to 10 minutes. Makes 8 servings.

Red Deviled Eggs

      6 hard-cooked eggs
      2 tablespoons mayonnaise or
         salad dressing
      1 teaspoon grated onion
      1 teaspoon prepared mustard
    ½ teaspoon Worcestershire sauce
      1 2¼-ounce can deviled ham
         Salt
         Pepper

Cut tops off eggs; remove yolks and mash. Mix with mayonnaise, onion, mustard, Worcestershire sauce, and deviled ham. Add salt and pepper to taste. Fill eggs with deviled mixture, using pastry tube, if desired. Makes 12.

Deviled Hamburgers

    ⅓ cup chili sauce
      1 tablespoon chopped onion
      1 teaspoon prepared horseradish
      1 teaspoon prepared mustard
    ½ teaspoon Worcestershire sauce
      1 pound ground beef
      8 slices bread

Combine first 5 ingredients and ¾ teaspoon salt. Add ground beef; mix well. Trim crusts from bread slices; toast one side. Spread each untoasted side with ¼ cup meat; spread to edges. Broil 5 to 6 minutes. Serves 4.

Hot Deviled Potatoes

         Packaged instant mashed
            potatoes (enough for 4
            servings)
       ½ cup dairy sour cream
               •   •   •
         2 teaspoons prepared mustard
       ½ teaspoon salt
       ½ teaspoon sugar
         2 tablespoons chopped green onion

Prepare potatoes according to package directions. Heat sour cream (do not boil). Add mustard, salt, and sugar; stir to blend. Mix into hot potatoes with onion. Turn into 1-quart casserole. Sprinkle with paprika, if desired. Bake at 350° about 10 minutes. Serves 5.

Deviled Swiss Steak

  ¼ cup all-purpose flour
1½ teaspoons dry mustard
  1 3-pound beef round steak,
       1½ inches thick
  ¼ cup salad oil
  1 tablespoon Worcestershire sauce
  1 3-ounce can mushroom crowns,
       drained (½ cup)
     Butter or margarine

Combine flour, 2 teaspoons salt, mustard, and ¼ teaspoon pepper. Sprinkle mixture over meat; pound in with meat mallet. In heavy skillet brown steak slowly on both sides in hot oil. Combine ½ cup water and Worcestershire; add to meat. Cover tightly and cook over very low heat till tender, about 1¾ to 2 hours.

Remove steak to platter. Heat mushrooms in a little butter; serve with steak. Skim fat from meat juices; serve juices with steak. Garnish with parsley, if desired. Serves 6 to 8.

DEVILED HAM—A canned mixture of ground or minced fully cooked ham and seasonings. Deviled ham makes a convenient sandwich spread, or it can be the basis for appetizers and main dishes.

Deviled Ham-Bean Bake

  1 16-ounce can pork and beans
       in tomato sauce
  1 8-ounce can tomatoes, well
       drained (½ cup)
  1 4½-ounce can deviled ham
  ½ cup chopped onion
  1 tablespoon molasses
  1 teaspoon prepared mustard
     Dash salt

Combine pork and beans, tomatoes, ham, onion, molasses, mustard, and salt in a 1-quart casserole and bake, uncovered, at 350° for 1½ hours. Makes 6 servings.

Deviled Swiss Steak cooks to ideal juiciness and tenderness due to slow braising in a Worcestershire sauce and dry mustard-spiced liquid. Garnish with mushroom crowns and parsley.

Deviled Ham and Tuna Sandwiches

A hearty sandwich filling—

- 1 6½- or 7-ounce can tuna, drained and flaked
- 1 4½-ounce can deviled ham
- 3 hard-cooked eggs, chopped
- ¼ cup finely chopped celery
- 2 tablespoons chopped dill pickle
- ½ teaspoon grated onion
- ⅓ cup mayonnaise or salad dressing
- 16 slices white bread
  Softened butter or margarine
  Lettuce leaves

Combine tuna, deviled ham, eggs, celery, dill pickle, and onion; blend in mayonnaise. Chill. Spread bread on one side with softened butter; spread 8 of the slices on buttered side with tuna mixture. Top each with lettuce leaf, then bread, buttered side down. Makes 8 servings.

DEVIL'S FOOD CAKE—A light-textured chocolate cake with a deep mahogany color. The name seems to have been attached to this cake in order to contrast its dark chocolate color with the delicate whiteness of an angel food cake. Devil's food cake differs from regular chocolate cake in that it contains more baking soda and has a more pronounced chocolate flavor and a darker chocolate color.

Many homemakers marvel at the rich, red appearance achieved from some devil's food cake recipes. This redness can be influenced by several ingredients. A deeper red is attained by using sweet rather than sour milk. Although an increase in baking soda darkens the color, an excess will make the cake taste alkaline and bitter. The quantity of chocolate used as well as its brand will also affect devil's food cake color. Some recipes, furthermore, include a small amount of red food coloring to enhance color. (See also *Cake.*)

The long-time favorite Devil's Food Cake wears a party-pretty boiled frosting variation, Peppermint-Stick Frosting. A splash of crunchy candy tidbits dresses the frosty top and sides.

Devil's Food Cake

    ⅔ cup shortening
    2¼ cups sifted cake flour
    1¾ cups sugar
    1 teaspoon salt
    1 teaspoon baking soda
    1 teaspoon baking powder
    1 cup milk
        • • •
    ¼ cup milk
    3 eggs
    3 1-ounce squares unsweetened
        chocolate, melted and cooled
    1 teaspoon red food coloring
        Peppermint-Stick Frosting

Place shortening in mixer bowl. Sift cake flour, sugar, salt, baking soda, and baking powder. Add the 1 cup milk; mix batter until flour is moistened. Beat mixture 2 minutes at medium speed on electric mixer.

Add remaining ¼ cup milk, eggs, chocolate, and red food coloring. Beat 2 minutes longer. Bake in 2 greased and lightly floured 9x1½-inch round pans at 350° for 35 to 40 minutes. Cool. Frost with *Peppermint-Stick Frosting:* Place 2 unbeaten egg whites, 1½ cups sugar, 2 teaspoons light corn syrup *or* ¼ teaspoon cream of tartar, ⅓ cup cold water, and dash salt in top of double boiler (don't place over boiling water); beat ½ minute at low speed on electric mixer. Place over boiling water, but not touching water. Cook, beating constantly, till frosting forms stiff peaks, *about* 7 minutes (*don't overcook*). Remove from boiling water.

If desired, pour into mixing bowl. Add 1 teaspoon vanilla and few drops red food coloring; beat till of spreading consistency, about 2 minutes. Frost tops and sides of cake layers. Trim cake with crushed peppermint-stick candy.

Red Devil's Food Cake

    ½ cup shortening
    1¾ cups sugar
    1 teaspoon vanilla
    3 eggs, separated
    2½ cups sifted cake flour
    ½ cup unsweetened cocoa powder
    1½ teaspoons baking soda
    1 teaspoon salt
    1⅓ cups cold water

Cream shortening and *1 cup* of the sugar till light and fluffy. Add vanilla and egg yolks, one at a time, beating well after each. Sift together sifted cake flour, unsweetened cocoa powder, baking soda, and salt; add to creamed mixture alternately with cold water, beating well after each addition.

Beat egg whites till soft peaks form; gradually add the remaining ¾ cup sugar, beating till stiff peaks form. Fold egg whites into cake batter; blend well. Pour into 2 greased and lightly floured 9x1½-inch round pans. Bake at 350° for 30 to 35 minutes.

Devilicious Cherry Cake

A fluffy cream cheese topping and wine-sparked cherry sauce round out this elegant dessert—

    1 package 2-layer-size devil's
        food cake mix
        • • •
    1 16-ounce can pitted dark sweet
        cherries
    ¼ cup sugar
    2 tablespoons cornstarch
    ¼ cup red Burgundy
        • • •
    1 8-ounce package cream cheese,
        softened
    ¼ cup sugar
    2 tablespoons milk
    ¼ teaspoon vanilla

Prepare devil's food cake mix and bake in a 13x9x2-inch baking pan following package directions. Cool thoroughly.

Drain dark sweet cherries, reserving syrup. In saucepan blend the first ¼ cup sugar and cornstarch; gradually add reserved cherry syrup, mixing well. Cook and stir over medium heat till syrup mixture is thickened and bubbly. Remove cherry sauce from heat; stir in red Burgundy wine and drained dark sweet cherries. Keep sauce warm while the topping is being prepared.

Beat softened cream cheese till fluffy. Add remaining ¼ cup sugar, milk, and vanilla; beat with rotary beater or electric mixer till fluffy. Cut devil's food cake into squares. Top with a small mound of cream cheese mixture. Then spoon warm sweet cherry sauce over each serving. Makes 12 servings.

DEVONSHIRE CREAM *(dev' uhn shir)*—A clotted cream that was originally made in Devonshire County, England. The thick clots are obtained after fresh non-homogenized milk is left to stand for up to six hours, then slowly heated for one hour. The top layer of cream which forms is then skimmed off.

Devonshire cream is a highly regarded complement for fresh fruits, toast, and desserts. It is appropriately served at breakfast, lunch, or dinner and as the appetizer or dessert course.

Mock Strawberries Devonshire

1 3-ounce package cream cheese, softened
2 tablespoons sugar
1 cup whipping cream
   Fresh whole strawberries

In small mixer bowl combine cream cheese, sugar, dash salt, and *2 tablespoons* of the whipping cream; beat till fluffy. Whip remaining cream; fold into cream cheese mixture. Serve with fresh strawberries. Good for appetizer or dessert. Makes 1¾ cups.

DEWBERRY—A type of blackberry that grows on trailing rather than the traditional climbing vines. Although native to North America, species of dewberries are now found in many other parts of the world. Dewberries ripen a few weeks before their relatives, the standard blackberries. (See also *Blackberry*.)

DEXTRIN—An edible substance that possesses characteristics partway between starch and sugar. Dextrins are formed by the chemical action of heat, enzymes, or acids on starch. When starch or flour is pan-browned (heated without liquid), dextrins are formed. In the digestion of starches to sugar, starches are first changed to dextrins by enzymes. Corn syrup, commercially produced by allowing cornstarch and acid to react, contains numerous dextrins.

Pure dextrins are white, but those used in most home cooking are yellow to brown. Dextrins prepared by pan-browning flour or starch are often used when making gravy to improve the sauce color. The gravy mixture will not, however, be as thick as when plain flour or starch is used.

DEXTROSE—A simple sugar that is found widely in fruits, honey, and some vegetables. Dextrose may be called glucose or fruit sugar interchangeably.

Dextrose is only about three-fourths as sweet as table sugar. Because it is easy to digest, dextrose is used for intravenous feeding. (See also *Sugar*.)

DHAL, DHALL *(dül)*—A purée, thick or thin in consistency, made from legumes or beans. *Dhal* is a common food eaten as a vegetable in India and the East Indies. Its appearance is reminiscent of a porridge. (See also *Indian Cookery*.)

DIABLE *(dē ä' bl)*—1. The French word for deviled. 2. A cooking utensil made of two earthenware pans, one of which rests inside the other. 3. An accompaniment sauce for meat, poultry, or fish. Diable sauce is made by adding white wine, vinegar, onion, and spices to a basic brown sauce.

Sauce Diable

¼ cup snipped green onion
3 tablespoons dry white wine
8 to 10 whole peppercorns, crushed
½ cup Brown Sauce
½ teaspoon snipped parsley
½ teaspoon Worcestershire sauce

Combine green onion, wine, and peppercorns in saucepan. Reduce mixture to ½ its volume by boiling. Add Brown Sauce, parsley, and Worcestershire sauce. Heat through. Makes about ⅔ cup.

Brown Sauce: Melt 1½ tablespoons butter or margarine in saucepan; blend in 1½ tablespoons all-purpose flour. Cook and stir over low heat till browned. Stir in one 10½-ounce can condensed beef broth diluted with water to make 2 cups. Bring to boiling and cook 3 to 5 minutes. Reduce heat and simmer 30 minutes; stir occasionally. Makes 1⅓ cups. Use ½ cup as above. Refrigerate remainder; use as gravy.

DICE—To cut food into cubes about ⅛ to ¼ inch thick. A sharp knife is employed first to cut food into slices and then into strips. The strips are piled together and cut crosswise into small cubes. The diced food size may be indicated in a recipe ingredient list as "finely diced."

DIET—1. A person's daily food consumption. 2. The regulation of food consumption commonly associated with a trim figure.

For most people the word "diet" spells a horrendous picture of niggardly meals, watercress sandwiches, grapefruit, weak tea, and an absence of pastries. A diet, in fact, is a necessary balance of nutrients to maintain good health for everyone.

The nutrients come from foods of the Basic 4 Food Groups. The groups include meat, milk, vegetable-fruit, and bread-cereal. When these food groups are used by the body, they form heat energy in measured units called calories. Individual body build and daily activity influence the amount of calories which can be used up satisfactorily in one day. If the body consumes too much food, the calories formed are not used and, instead, form fatty tissue. Likewise, when too little food is consumed, the body uses up any fatty tissue it can, thus resulting in weight loss.

The principal food nutrients found within the Basic 4 Groups consist of carbohydrates, fats, proteins, vitamins, minerals, and water. Carbohydrates and fats are the energy foods, with fat contributing about twice as many calories as either carbohydrates or protein. The body building nutrient is protein of two sources—animal and vegetable. Vitamins and minerals are important to general body metabolism and operation. Water, furnishing no calories but some minerals, is important for body regulatory processes, so at least six glasses should be drunk each day.

Special weight programs and diets set up for health purposes require the guidance of a physician. Diets involving the gain or loss of weight are important to individuals learning to adopt better dietary habits. Nutrient diets, such as low-sodium, high-protein, or others must be guided by a physician so too much or too little of another nutrient is not being consumed.

Diced foods add contrast in shape to usual dishes. Use a French knife and wooden cutting board to cut food strips crosswise.

Complete formula diets, both solid and liquid, have become popular since their introduction by pharmaceutical companies and food manufacturers. Low-residue foods such as celery or lettuce should accompany formula diets to maintain bulk.

Dietary standards have been set up to quantitatively summarize nutritional requirements. A diet for good health can easily be established, but before going on a weight loss or weight gain diet, consult your physician. (See also *Nutrition*.)

DIETETIC FOOD *(di' i tet' ik)*—Commercially prepared food used in special diets. Examples of dietetic foods include low-sodium cheese and bread, tuna packed in water (without salt) instead of oil, and low-calorie dessert powders made with noncaloric sweeteners. Diabetic foods, not to be confused with dietetic foods, refer to a type of food that is sugar free, such as some artificial sweeteners.

DIGESTION—A body process occurring in the digestive tract by which food is broken into substances that can be absorbed and assimilated by the body. Digestion starts in the mouth where the food is chewed and mixed with saliva. This process continues as the food is acted upon chemically by digestive juices. The digested food reaches all tissues of the body by way of the bloodstream, thus furnishing body-building and maintenance materials.

Food temperatures have an effect on rate of digestion; warm foods speed up the process, while cold foods slow it down. Emotional stress and strain impede digestion; tranquility and happiness help digestion on its normal course.

DIJON MUSTARD *(dē zhön')*—A French-style mustard containing dry mustard, herbs, spices, and white wine. It originated in Dijon, France, and is considered by connoisseurs to be one of the finest mustards. Dijon mustard is available in jars at specialty food stores and markets. Its smooth, tart, yet pleasing, flavor is an excellent seasoning for eggs, soups, roasts, steaks, chops, and fish. (See also *Mustard.*)

Mustard 'n Ham Dip

Combine one 4-ounce package whipped cream cheese, one 2¼-ounce can deviled ham, 1½ teaspoons Dijon-style mustard, 1 tablespoon chopped chives, and 2 teaspoons milk. Chill well; serve with relishes, chips, and crackers.

DILL—An aromatic herb related to the parsley family. The word dill is derived from the Norse *dilla* meaning "to lull to sleep," and it was formerly given to infants for that reason. Dill was used by Babylonian and Assyrian doctors as a drug, and the pungent seed was also said to remedy a stomachache and other such ailments.

The Romans made crowns of the dillweed. Colonial settlers chewed dillseed during long church services to delay hunger. Bad breath was also believed to be eliminated by chewing dillseed, and ground dillseed was recommended for use to those on salt-free diets.

Native to the Mediterranean countries and southern Russia, dill still grows wild in parts of Asia and Africa and is widely cultivated in England, India, Germany, and Romania. Dill, popular in the United States, is grown commercially in the southern and eastern parts of the country and

also in some midwestern states. Dillweed is grown mainly in and around California.

The dill plant bears yellow blossoms which turn into tiny seeds. The mature plant is available, usually tied in bunches, in food stores and markets during the late summer and early autumn. The feathery, bright green leaves are dried, bottled, and labeled dillweed, and are found with bottled whole dillseed in the market.

Ground dill is bottled in ½- to 1-ounce containers and blends more easily with food than either the seed or dillweed. Dillseeds, in ½- to 2-ounce containers, have a warm, slightly sharp taste serving to stimulate the appetite, thus making them suitable for salad seasonings. Dillweed, either fresh or bottled, may garnish or enhance the flavor of mild foods.

Dill leaves are natural flavor additions to many foods. Add chopped dill to buttered new potatoes and to cream sauce for fish or shellfish; blend with cream or cottage cheese; sprinkle a bit on broiled meats or fish; or put a dash of dill in green salads or cooked green beans. If dillweed is used instead of fresh dill as a garnish, moisten it with a little lemon juice or water to revive its aromatic flavor.

Use dillseed with potatoes to flavor cabbage, in vegetable salads or slaws, or in

Tantalize guests with crisp zucchini sticks dipped in Dill Dip. As appetizer or relish, it will be the topic of conversation.

Spoon zesty Dill Sauce over Corned Beef Squares and cabbage wedges. The popular everyday dish becomes a new favorite.

soups and stews. Dill is the obvious flavor given to dill pickles. A few seeds add subtle flavor to the liquid in which fish is simmered or poached. The flavor of dillseed is found in a number of sausage and luncheon meats. (See also *Herbs*.)

Dill Dip

In small bowl combine one 3-ounce package cream cheese, softened; 1 tablespoon finely chopped pimiento-stuffed green olives; 1 teaspoon grated onion; 1/4 teaspoon dried dillweed; and dash salt. Mix well. Stir in 1 to 2 tablespoons light cream to make mixture of dipping consistency. Chill. Serve with zucchini sticks as an appetizer. Makes about 2/3 cup.

Corned Beef Squares with Dill Sauce

In medium mixing bowl combine 1 cup milk, 2 eggs, 1 cup coarsely crushed saltine crackers (about 22 crackers), 1/2 cup chopped onion, 1 tablespoon prepared horseradish, and 1 teaspoon dry mustard. Add two 12-ounce cans corned beef, chopped (4 cups) to mixture; mix thoroughly. Turn corned beef mixture into 10x6x1 1/2-inch baking dish. Bake at 375° for 30 to 35 minutes. Meanwhile, cut 1 medium head cabbage into 6 to 8 wedges. Prepare Dill Sauce. Cut corned beef into squares. Serve with cabbage and Dill Sauce. Serves 6 to 8.

Dill Sauce: In medium saucepan combine one 10 1/2-ounce can condensed cream of mushroom soup, 1/2 cup milk, 1 teaspoon dried dillweed, and 1 teaspoon dry mustard. Cook, stirring frequently, over medium heat till bubbly.

Dill Potatoes

Peel 1 1/2 pounds tiny new potatoes (about 15); cook in boiling salted water till tender, about 15 to 20 minutes; drain thoroughly. Melt 1 tablespoon butter or margarine; blend in 2 teaspoons all-purpose flour, 1/2 teaspoon salt, and 1 teaspoon snipped fresh dillweed. Add 1/3 cup milk and 3/4 cup light cream all at once. Cook and stir over medium heat till mixture thickens and bubbles. Reduce heat. Add cooked potatoes; heat through. Sprinkle with additional dillweed. Makes 4 or 5 servings.

Dublin Potato Salad

  2 tablespoons vinegar
  1 teaspoon celery seed
  1 teaspoon mustard seed
  3 medium-large potatoes
  2 teaspoons sugar
  2 cups finely shredded cabbage
  1 12-ounce can corned beef,
      chilled and cubed
 1/4 cup sliced green onion
 1/4 cup finely chopped dill pickle
  1 cup mayonnaise or salad
      dressing
 1/4 cup milk

Combine vinegar, celery seed, and mustard seed; set aside. Meanwhile, peel and cook potatoes in enough boiling salted water to cover till done, 30 to 40 minutes; drain and cube. While potatoes are still warm, drizzle with vinegar mixture. Sprinkle with sugar and 1/2 teaspoon salt; chill before serving.

Before serving, add cabbage, corned beef, onion, and pickle to potatoes. Combine mayonnaise, milk, and 1/2 teaspoon salt. Pour mayonnaise mixture over corned beef mixture and toss lightly. Makes 6 to 8 servings.

Dilly Hamburgers

In small bowl combine 1 cup dairy sour cream, 1 teaspoon prepared mustard, and 3 tablespoons snipped fresh dillweed. Form 1 to 1½ pounds ground beef into 4 to 6 patties, ½ inch thick. Broil patties over *hot* coals about 9 minutes; turn and sprinkle with salt and pepper to taste. Broil to desired doneness, about 6 minutes longer. Season again with salt and pepper. Serve on hot toasted buns. Top with Dill Sauce. Makes 6 to 8 servings.

DILUTE—To thin or to weaken the strength or flavor of a food substance by adding a liquid such as water to it.

DIP—1. Immersing food in a liquid or in a dry mixture, such as flour. 2. Savory soft or semiliquid food mixtures into which crisp crackers, potato chips, raw vegetables, or special snack foods are dipped. Typically American, dips became popular shortly after the end of World War II.

The dip base may be cream cheese, sour cream, sweet cream or prepared baby foods already chopped and puréed to save time and work. Flavor the creamy dip mixture with bacon bits, seafood, onions, pickles, dried soups, relish, dill, favorite herbs and spices, or delicacies, such as minced clams, avocados, or Roquefort cheese.

Dips, although similar to canapé fillings, have a softer consistency. They should be thick enough not to drip on clothing or carpet when food sticks or chips are dipped into them, but not so thick that the dip needs to be scooped out. Dips may be served hot or cold.

Beat additional sour cream, sweet cream, or milk into the dip if it becomes thick upon standing. Add the amount needed to bring the dip back to its proper consistency. Crackers, toast sticks, potato chips, corn chips, pretzels, or melba toast are ready-made, convenient scoops. Cut narrow toast strips or cookie cutter shapes for unusual bread variations.

Crisp, cold, raw vegetables, such as carrot and celery sticks, cauliflowerets, iced cucumber rounds, green pepper strips, mushrooms, and radishes, make delicious appetizer accompaniments to the dip. For party refreshments, surround a dip bowl with cooked shrimp or cocktail frankfurters. There are many uses for dips. They are most satisfactorily served to small, informal adult groups, such as a casual get-together, centered around a buffet meal, and as cocktail accompaniments. And the leftover dips make excellent dressings for a mixed green salad or the topping for hot vegetables. When mixed with minced meat, they are a good choice for use in sandwiches. (See also *Appetizer*.)

It is great snacking for weight watchers with Dieter's Dip. The quick-to-fix dip is served with chilled, cooked shrimp.

Make-ahead dip tips

So that the flavorings can mingle and mellow properly, prepare dips several hours before serving and refrigerate. Use strong spices such as garlic, onion, and chili powder sparingly because they intensify on standing.

Dieter's Dip

  1 12-ounce carton cottage
      cheese (1½ cups)
  ½ envelope dill dip mix
      (about 1 teaspoon)
      . . .
  1 tablespoon finely diced
      canned pimiento
  1 tablespoon snipped parsley
      Chilled cooked shrimp

Beat cottage cheese and dill dip mix together with electric mixer. Stir in pimiento and snipped parsley. Serve with chilled shrimp.

Hot Cheese and Crab Dip

 10 ounces sharp natural
      Cheddar cheese
  8 ounces sharp process
      American cheese
  ⅓ cup milk
  ½ cup dry white wine
  1 7½-ounce can crab meat, drained,
      flaked, and cartilage removed

Cut cheeses in small pieces; combine in a saucepan with milk. Stir over low heat till cheeses melt. Stir in wine and crab; heat through. Serve in chafing dish with shredded wheat wafers, if desired. Makes 3 cups.

Dip à la Spaghetti

  1 tablespoon dry spaghetti
      sauce mix
  1 tablespoon finely chopped
      green pepper
  1 cup dairy sour cream

Stir spaghetti sauce mix and green pepper into dairy sour cream. Chill. Serve with crisp vegetables or corn chips, if desired.

Special late evening snack

← Surround piping Hot Cheese and Crab Dip with shredded wheat wafers, garnished with parsley and crab, and tempt your guests.

Lobster Dip Elegante

Crisp crackers or toast dunked in hot lobster dip are a welcome change-of-pace party treat—

  1 8-ounce package cream cheese
  ¼ cup mayonnaise or salad
      dressing
  1 clove garlic, crushed
  1 teaspoon grated onion
  1 teaspoon prepared mustard
  1 teaspoon sugar
      Dash seasoned salt
  1 5-ounce can lobster, flaked
      (about 1 cup)
  3 tablespoons sauterne

Melt cream cheese over low heat, stirring constantly. Blend in mayonnaise or salad dressing, garlic, onion, mustard, sugar, and salt. Stir in flaked lobster and sauterne; heat through. Serve hot with melba toast and assorted crackers, if desired. Makes 1¾ cups.

Chicken Liver-Onion Dip

Easy onion soup and liver dip served with crackers will delight any dip-loving crowd—

  ¼ cup water
  2 tablespoons dry onion soup mix
  ½ pound chicken livers
  1 hard-cooked egg, sliced
  ¼ cup mayonnaise or salad
      dressing
  ½ teaspoon Worcestershire sauce
  3 slices bacon, crisp-cooked,
      drained, and crumbled

Combine water and dry onion soup mix; set aside. Meanwhile, in small saucepan simmer chicken livers in water till tender, about 8 to 10 minutes. Drain; cool. Place onion soup mixture, livers, egg, mayonnaise, and Worcestershire sauce in electric blender container; cover and blend till almost smooth.

Or, put livers and egg through meat grinder. Combine onion soup mixture, Worcestershire sauce, and mayonnaise or salad dressing. Stir in liver mixture; mix well. Stir in about two-thirds of the bacon; chill thoroughly. Top mixture with remaining crumbled bacon; serve with assorted crackers or corn chips.

DISSOLVE—To release a dry substance into a liquid, thus forming a solution. A food ingredient may be stirred or melted into the liquid as part of a food preparation procedure. Examples include: stirring sugar in water to make syrup, sugar dissolved in hot coffee for flavor, gelatin in water, salt in a sauce, or yeast in water.

DISTILLED LIQUOR—Beverages of high alcoholic content produced by separating alcohol from another product. This is achieved by heating an alcohol-water mixture to a temperature between the boiling point of alcohol and water at which time the alcohol vaporizes. The vapors may be recondensed into a pure alcohol liquid form with special equipment.

Although distillation is based on the fact that the boiling point of water is lower than that of alcohol, the distillation of liquors involves more than just heating the alcohol-water mixture. This is especially true of brandy, distilled from wine; rum from molasses or other sugar-cane products; whiskey distilled from grain; and gin and vodka which are produced from any one of a number of products including wheat or rye. (See also *Liquor.*)

DISTILLED WATER—Purified water made by condensing the steam of boiling water. The vapor is condensed into pure water and has a flat taste due to the absence of air and natural chemical salts. The distilled product can be aerated to remove this flat taste for drinking purposes.

Distilled water is used on steamships for drinking purposes. It is also used extensively in steam irons and for cleaning equipment and glassware used in factories and chemical laboratories. Doctors recommend distilled water to make baby's formula. The water should be stored in tightly covered containers to avoid contamination and to retain its purity.

DIVAN (*dī' van*)—A recipe style created in a New York restaurant for a luscious, baked dish of chicken breasts, broccoli, and a rich, creamy sauce. The name is now given to similar mixtures with meats used instead of chicken breasts, such as veal or ham. It closely resembles a casserole.

Classic Chicken Divan

2 10-ounce packages frozen
   broccoli spears
¼ cup butter or margarine
6 tablespoons all-purpose flour
2 cups chicken broth
½ cup whipping cream
3 tablespoons dry white wine
. . .
3 chicken breasts, halved
   and cooked
¼ cup grated Parmesan cheese

Cook broccoli according to package directions; drain. Melt butter or margarine; blend in flour, ½ teaspoon salt, and dash pepper. Add chicken broth; cook and stir till mixture thickens and bubbles. Stir in cream and wine.

Place broccoli crosswise in 12x7½x2-inch baking dish. Pour *half* the sauce over. Top with chicken. To remaining sauce, add cheese; pour over chicken; sprinkle with additional Parmesan cheese. Bake at 350° till heated through, about 20 minutes. Then broil just till sauce is golden, about 5 minutes. Serves 6.

Easy Chicken Divan

2 10-ounce packages frozen
   broccoli spears
2 cups sliced cooked chicken
   or 3 chicken breasts,
   cooked and boned
2 10½-ounce cans condensed
   cream of chicken soup
¾ cup mayonnaise or salad
   dressing
1 teaspoon lemon juice
2 ounces sharp process American
   cheese, shredded (½ cup)
1 cup soft bread crumbs
1 tablespoon butter, melted

Cook broccoli according to package directions in salted water till tender; drain. Arrange broccoli in greased 12x7½x2-inch baking dish. Layer chicken atop the broccoli.

Combine next 3 ingredients; pour over chicken. Sprinkle with cheese. Combine crumbs and butter; sprinkle over all. Bake at 350° till heated, about 35 minutes. Trim with pimiento strips, if desired. Makes 6 to 8 servings.

Easy Chicken Divan, appropriately named as frozen broccoli and mushroom soup, combines with chicken to make an easy super-supper dish. Garnish with bright red pimiento strips.

DIVINITY—A fudgelike candy made with corn syrup, sugar, and water cooked to the hard-ball stage and then beaten into stiff-peaked egg whites. Divinity, sometimes called divinity fudge, is classified as a crystalline candy but is different from most crystalline candies because it contains egg whites. The candy is very similar to nougat which contains almonds and honey although nougat is heavier than divinity.

Because good divinity requires constant heavy beating (when electric mixer is not used) and since it sets very fast, it is more fun, and makes the job easier to make divinity with a partner.

Divinity may be stirred over hot water if it does not set. Hot water may be added to the candy if it becomes too hard to work. Candies using water instead of milk can be heated to a higher temperature as there is no danger of scorching. Reaching and maintaining the recommended candy temperature or cooking stage is very important to the consistency and texture of the cooked candy. Divinity should be cooked to the hard-ball stage, between 250° and 266°. The candy syrup will form a hard ball, yet will remain somewhat pliable.

High humidity or rainy weather may affect the setting up and keeping qualities of the candy. Cook the candy a degree or two higher if the humidity is high.

Wipe the sides of the pan occasionally with a damp brush to avoid crystal formation during cooking. Tint divinity with drops of food coloring to brighten dishes of assorted candy, and add nutmeats, candied fruits, or coconut during the last few strokes of beating before the divinity has a chance to cool and set thoroughly.

Fill up the candy plate with Remarkable Fudge squares topped with walnut half (See *Fudge*), white Divinity, Cherry Fluff Divinity, and Creamy Praline Patties (See *Praline*).

After all ingredients are mixed and beaten along with egg whites, drop divinity by spoonfuls onto waxed paper and leave it to cool. Additional nuts and toppings may be pressed into the top at this time. The light candy can also be turned into a buttered pan and cut into squares or pieces like fudge after it has set.

Eat divinity while it is fresh as it does not keep well and dries out quickly. Store fresh divinity in tightly covered containers. Divinities can be satisfactorily frozen.

Another candy made in the same way as divinity, but called seafoam, uses brown sugar instead of granulated sugar. This changes not only the flavor of the candy, but also its color. (See also *Candy*.)

Divinity

2½ cups sugar
½ cup light corn syrup
· · ·
2 egg whites
1 teaspoon vanilla

In 2-quart saucepan combine sugar, corn syrup, ¼ teaspoon salt, and ½ cup water. Cook to hard-ball stage (260°) stirring only till sugar dissolves. Beat egg whites to stiff peaks. Gradually pour syrup over egg whites, beating at high speed on electric mixer. Add vanilla; beat till candy holds its shape, 4 to 5 minutes. Quickly drop from teaspoon onto waxed paper. Makes about 40 pieces of divinity.

Cherry Fluff Divinity

Sweet pink confections studded with candied cherries are bound to tempt any candy dish taster—

2 cups sugar
½ cup water
¼ cup light corn syrup
1 7¼-ounce package fluffy
   cherry frosting mix
1 teaspoon vanilla
⅓ cup finely chopped red
   candied cherries

In a heavy 2-quart saucepan, combine sugar, water, and corn syrup. Cook and stir over medium heat till sugar dissolves and mixture is boiling. Cook, without stirring, to hard-ball stage (265°). Remove from heat. Meanwhile, prepare frosting mix according to package directions; transfer to large mixer bowl. *Very slowly* pour hot syrup over frosting, beating constantly at high speed on electric mixer, about 5 minutes. Continue beating 5 minutes more; stir in vanilla and cherries. Cool, stirring occasionally, till mixture holds soft peaks and begins to lose gloss. Drop mixture from rounded tablespoons onto waxed paper, swirling tops with spoon. Makes about 30 pieces.

Rainbow Divinity

Delicate divinity made new and colorful with flavored gelatin and tinted coconut—

3 cups sugar
¾ cup light corn syrup
¾ cup hot water
¼ teaspoon salt
   • • •
2 egg whites
½ 3-ounce package cherry- or lime-
   flavored gelatin* (3 tablespoons)
1 teaspoon vanilla
1 cup chopped nuts (optional)
¾ cup flaked coconut, tinted
   pink or green**

Butter sides of heavy 2-quart saucepan. In it combine sugar, corn syrup, water, and salt. Cook and stir till sugar dissolves and mixture reaches boiling point. Cook to hard-ball stage (250°) without stirring; remove from heat.

Push divinity from spoon onto waxed paper-lined baking sheet with the aid of another spoon. Candy is best when eaten fresh.

Meanwhile, beat egg whites to soft peaks; gradually add gelatin, beating to stiff peaks. Add vanilla and pour hot syrup slowly over egg white mixture, beating with mixer at high speed till soft peaks form and mixture starts to lose its gloss. Stir in nuts. Drop from teaspoon onto waxed paper. Sprinkle candy with tinted coconut. Makes about 54 pieces.

*Add few drops green food coloring to lime-flavored gelatin, if desired.

**Tint coconut by shaking with a few drops of food coloring in screw-top jar.

DOBOS TORTE (*dō' bōs, -bōsh*)—A Hungarian cake of butter cream-filled layers and a caramel topping. Josef Dobos, a Hungarian pastry chef, created this dessert confection, and is popular in Vienna.

The rich, butter cream filling, between each thin sponge cake layer, is usually chocolate. The topping may be whipped cream or a frosting but is most often a caramel glaze. Sometimes the whole cake is frosted, but this detracts from the superb torte attractiveness. Speed is necessary when making this Hungarian specialty with caramel topping. If the topping cools before servings have been cut, the caramel will crack and cannot be cut into even, neat slices. (See also *Torte.*)

Split cake layers in half using wooden picks as guides. Position picks in center of side all the way around. Slice.

Spread creamy chocolate filling with shaved chocolate between each cake layer. Position each layer with the cut side down.

Shortcut Dobos Torte

   5 eggs
 ½ teaspoon salt
   1 teaspoon vanilla
   1 cup granulated sugar
 1½ cups pancake mix
        • • •
   2 cups whipping cream
 ½ teaspoon vanilla
 ¼ cup sifted confectioners'
        sugar
 ¼ cup unsweetened cocoa powder
   2 1-ounce squares semisweet
        chocolate, shaved
 ¼ cup slivered almonds, toasted

Combine eggs, salt, and 1 teaspoon vanilla. Beat till thick and lemon-colored, about 5 minutes. Gradually beat in the granulated sugar; fold in pancake mix. Pour into 2 greased and waxed paper-lined 9x1½-inch round cake pans. Bake at 350° for 15 to 18 minutes. Cool; remove from pans. Split cake layers (see picture). To make filling, combine whipping cream, ½ teaspoon vanilla, confectioners' sugar, and cocoa powder; whip till thickened.

To assemble torte place cake layer on serving plate, *cut side down.* Spread with 1 cup of the whipped filling; sprinkle with about 1 tablespoon of the shaved chocolate. Top with second layer, cut side down; spread with same amounts of filling and shaved chocolate. Repeat with remaining 2 layers. Sprinkle toasted almonds on top layer. Chill before serving.

Elegant prepare-ahead dessert

New Shortcut Dobos Torte uses pancake→ mix to make spongy layers. Garnish with toasted almonds and shaved chocolate.

DOCK—A pungent herb, related to sorrel and buckwheat. The leaves are used in cooking to enhance and add to the flavor of foods.

Some varieties of dock plants grow wild and can, in fact, be a problem weed. The leaves are most desirable for cooking in the springtime when they still are young and tender. (See also *Herb*.)

DOLLOP—A recipe term describing a small amount, such as a scoop or spoonful, of semiliquid food used to garnish another food. A dollop of whipped cream can top a dessert or fruit salad. Likewise, a dollop of sour cream might dress and add flavor to a main dish, salad, or dessert.

DOLMA—A ground meat appetizer or main dish from the Near East. The word *dolma* literally means "something stuffed."

Traditionally, meat (usually lamb or mutton) together with rice, onion, and seasonings is wrapped in cabbage or grape leaves. However, other meat mixtures used as stuffing for vegetables, such as green peppers or squash, are frequently called *dolmas* also. The Greek form of *dolmas* wrapped in grape leaves are called *dolmades*. (See also *Greek Cookery*.)

Dollops of frozen whipped cream are helpful standbys for a quick topping. Freeze on cookie sheet, then transfer to a plastic bag.

Turkish Zucchini Dolmas

1 pound ground beef
⅓ cup uncooked packaged
    precooked rice
¾ cup milk
½ cup chopped onion
1 teaspoon salt
1 teaspoon chopped fresh mint
    or ¼ teaspoon dried mint
    leaves, crushed, *or* 1 teaspoon
    chopped fresh dillweed, *or* ¼
    teaspoon dried dillweed
¼ teaspoon pepper
2 pounds zucchini squash
    (5 medium)
2 8-ounce cans tomato sauce
½ teaspoon salt

Combine ground beef, uncooked rice, milk, chopped onion, the 1 teaspoon salt, mint *or* dillweed, and pepper; mix well. Cut both ends from zucchini squash. With apple corer, scoop out centers of zucchini. (Chop centers and reserve.) Fill zucchini loosely with ground meat mixture. Make meatballs from leftover meat mixture.

In a large skillet combine tomato sauce, the ½ teaspoon salt, and reserved chopped zucchini centers; heat through. Add zucchini and ground meatballs. Cover and simmer till done, about 30 minutes. Makes 4 to 6 servings.

DOT—To cover the surface of food with small pieces of another food, for example, to place bits of butter over pie fruit filling.

DOUBLE-ACTING BAKING POWDER—A leavening compound which releases part of the carbon dioxide at room temperature and the remainder during baking. This is the most common type used in home kitchens. (See also *Baking Powder*.)

DOUBLE BOILER—A utensil comprised of two saucepans, one of which rests inside the other. The top pan contains the food; the bottom pan, water. (The water should not touch the bottom of the top pan.) Thus, the food cooks by indirect heat produced as the heated water changes to steam.

The double boiler cooking method is very satisfactory when controlled temperatures below boiling are needed. The water in the bottom pan is usually heated to just below boiling. Heat-sensitive sauces and egg mixtures such as hollandaise sauce or stirred custard are often cooked over hot water to prevent curdling. Semisweet chocolate pieces must be melted over hot water; if boiling water were used, steam from the water might cause the chocolate to solidify. To melt commercially made caramels, the candies must also be melted in a double boiler to avoid scorching.

DOUBLE CONSOMMÉ — 1. A consommé that has been cooked down to concentrate and strengthen its flavor. 2. A standard consommé to which bouillon cubes are added. Canned condensed consommé, if left undiluted, may also be used as a double consommé. (See also *Consommé*.)

DOUBLE CRÈME CHEESE — A rich, soft cheese produced in France. Several varieties of double crèmes are made in different areas of France. All are high in milk fat — a 60 percent concentration by law. These high-fat cheeses are made by adding cream before and after the whey is removed from the milk.

Double crèmes may be purchased in the fresh or ripened form. Except for their double richness and prominent tangy taste, the fresh double crème varieties are very similar to American cream cheeses.

Cured or ripened double crèmes undergo more processing than do the fresh cheeses. They are brushed with special molds and then allowed to ripen from exterior to interior. This ripening action takes from 10 days to 2 weeks. The resulting products are again rich and tangy in taste but are heavier in texture, somewhat reminiscent of rich cheesecake.

Because of the increased milk fat present, double crème cheeses deteriorate rapidly even with refrigeration. For this reason, only a few varieties are available in the United States, frequently only at specialty cheese shops or delicatessens.

Be very careful when selecting double crèmes. First, choose a reputable store. Second, check the wrapping; it should look clean and fresh, not brown and sticky. Third, check for odor. A strong odor indicates that the cheese is old.

DOUBLE GLOUCESTER CHEESE *(glos' tuhr)* — A hard, satiny cheese. Golden in color and mellow, but slightly piquant in flavor, double Gloucester cheese was originally made from the rich milk of Gloucester cows only. Today, however, milk from other breeds of cows is used.

Double Gloucester is a centuries-old English favorite formed into large circles called millstones. These millstones are thick and heavy, and are aged six months to one year. (Regular Gloucester is made in thinner circles that are aged six weeks.) The millstones are cut generally into small wedges for retail sale.

Double Gloucester makes a delightfully different addition to a cheese appetizer or dessert tray. (See also *Gloucester Cheese*.)

DOUGH — A mixture containing flour, liquid, seasonings, and usually a leavening agent. A dough is firm enough to work with the hands or knead. In fact, the word dough comes from the Old English word *dah* meaning "to knead." This thick, nonpourable state distinguishes it from batters.

Doughs can be divided into two basic categories: soft and stiff doughs. Soft doughs contain about one part liquid to three parts flour. They feel soft but can still be handled on a floured surface. Typical soft dough recipes are baking powder biscuits, yeast rolls, and yeast breads.

The composition of stiff doughs, on the other hand, is approximately one part liquid to four parts flour. The high proportion of flour produces a dough that is firm to the touch and can be rolled easily. Piecrust, homemade noodle, and rolled cookie doughs all fall in the stiff dough classification. (See also *Batter*.)

Double Gloucester, an English cheese.

DOUGHNUT — Small, individual sweet cakes leavened with baking powder or yeast and cooked by deep-fat frying or baking. They are often dusted with sugar, glazed with a sweet icing, or filled.

Light, puffy fried cakes with holes have been eaten since the earliest of times. Some have even been found in petrified form among prehistoric Indian ruins.

A product of pioneer cooking, the first real doughnuts were introduced to America by the Dutch settlers in New England. These were yeast-raised spherical doughnuts. Because they were called fried cakes by the early New Englanders, upstate New Yorkers still refer to doughnuts as fried cakes. Today, doughnut specialty shops are popular all over the country.

The doughnuts, called oil cakes by the Dutch, became an integral part of pre-fasting activity. The Pennsylvania Dutch served triangular yeast-raised doughnuts called *fastnacht kuche* the day before Lent, Fastnacht Day or Shrove Tuesday. The custom developed with the thrifty Dutch woman who used up all the butters and fats, which were not allowed during the Lenten season, in the doughnut recipe. The last person down to breakfast in the morning on Fastnacht Day was called a "lazy fastnacht," assigned extra work duties for the day, and only received one large *fastnacht kuche* to eat.

A sea captain is credited with cutting the hole in the doughnut, sometime during the middle of the nineteenth century. He complained of the doughy uncooked center and how difficult it was to digest. The sea captain asked that the center of the doughnut be cut out. The cook liked the easier method of cooking and the captain enjoyed the holed doughnut. Thus, to the delight of children and coffee drinkers, the warm, holed doughnut was born. Or so the story goes of how the hole was cut in the doughnut and still remains.

Before airtight wrappings and containers were developed, leftover doughnuts became hard and dried out in a very short time. Thrifty homemakers found that dunking doughnuts in coffee softened them and made an excellent snack. This led to the widespread popularity of the doughnut and coffee companionship.

Types of doughnuts: The basic doughnut can take on round, square, triangular, and braided shapes. These shapes are often a part of the doughnut's name.

Crullers, or twisted doughnuts, are made with more eggs than the usual doughnut recipe, producing a lighter, richer product with a moist texture.

Round or square doughnuts without a hole in the center are actually breads fried in deep fat on the range. Jelly-filled Bismarcks were named after a German politician. French doughnuts differ from basic doughnut recipes in that cream puff dough rather than a yeast dough is used to form the doughnut rings in the hot fat.

Purchase packaged ready-made doughnuts at the supermarket or buy the exact amount wanted at a local bakery or specialty shop. There is usually a selection of plain, glazed, sugared, and filled types.

How to store: Keep fresh doughnuts in a tightly covered container to avoid drying out. To make leftover doughnuts soft and fresh, place them in a paper bag or covered container and heat in a warm oven. Package the number of doughnuts to be eaten at one time in moisture-vaporproof material and freeze for future use.

Basic preparation: The proportion of the ingredients to each other has a great effect upon the finished doughnut. The most important variations include the liquid, fat, and sugar. Too much of any one of these, particularly the sugar, causes greater fat absorption by the doughnut during the deep-fat frying process.

Whole eggs as well as egg yolks are required in most doughnut recipes. Whole eggs make light, puffy doughnuts, while additional egg yolks contribute extra richness. The best flour with which to make ideal doughnuts is a blend of bread flour and cake or pastry flour.

Pick a favorite doughnut

Choose New Orleans Square Doughnuts, →
Coconut Cake or Potato Doughnuts, Doughnut Balls or Filled Doughnuts, or Crullers.

When making doughnuts, keep dough soft and pliable by using as little flour as possible during rolling. Avoid overhandling the dough at all times to eliminate the possibility of producing a tough product with a compact texture. The dough may be chilled slightly in the refrigerator before rolling to make the cutting easier.

Roll the chilled dough to one-third inch thickness and cut with a floured doughnut cutter. Cookie and biscuit cutters can be used to make interesting shapes. A quick and easy way to make doughnuts is to cut the centers from convenient refrigerated biscuits and deep-fat fry as usual. Drop the centers in to fry for the youngsters.

A baking powder dough may be allowed to stand, uncovered, for a few minutes before frying to allow a delicate thin crust to form. This will inhibit the immediate absorption of fat. Doughnuts made with yeast must be allowed to double in size after cutting before they are fried.

When the doughnuts are dropped into the hot fat, they will sink to the bottom and then rise and float. After the doughnut has risen to the top, turn with fork till both sides are evenly browned. Turn some doughnuts several times to prevent surface from cracking. The complete frying time should not be over three minutes. Remove doughnut from hot fat with fork or slotted spoon. Lay doughnuts on paper toweling to absorb excess fat. The cooked doughnut should be evenly browned and have a light texture throughout.

A wide variety of choices exist at this point as to whether the doughnut should be served filled, spiced, or frosted. Serve jelly-filled Bismarcks to the morning coffee group or for Sunday breakfast. Make a slit in the side of the uncooked doughnut that has been cut with a biscuit cutter. Insert the jam with a spoon or squirt the jelly in with a long, narrow pastry tube. Jelly can also be sandwiched between two dough rounds and deep-fat fried.

For afternoon or evening eating, prepare whipped cream doughnuts or frosted, twisted crullers. Cut doughnuts in half spreading one half with whipped cream and top with the second half. Garnish whipped cream doughnuts with fruits and nuts. They can also be filled with jelly or custard. The Danish use a special aebleskiver pan for making their round doughnuts and then use applesauce and cream for the rich filling to serve for dessert.

Make interesting shapes with rich cruller dough and spread with mouth-watering frostings. Dunk the frosted doughnuts in little dishes containing coconut or small decorative colored candies.

Doughnuts can be sprinkled with granulated sugar, confectioners' sugar, or a cinnamon and sugar mixture. An easy way to completely cover the doughnuts is to drop them, one at a time, in a paper bag with sugar, then shake gently.

Aside from the traditional warm, sugary doughnut, many doughnut variations can be concocted with fillings and unusual ingredients. Fold the doughnut dough over a pitted prune or other dried fruit before deep-fat frying. Mix snipped dates and raisins into dough to make fruited balls. Added mashed potatoes or sweet potatoes give an interesting flavor to the balls.

Leftover doughnuts make an excellent coffee companion, or serve them with hot apple cider for a change. Perfect for dunk-

---

Doughnut frying pointers

Maintaining the hot fat at a temperature between 350° and 375° is best for frying doughnuts. When the fat is below this temperature, the doughnuts may become fat soaked, making them greasy to the taste and difficult to digest. Too hot a deep-fat temperature will cook the outside of the doughnut too quickly while leaving the inside of it uncooked.

If a fat thermometer, automatic fryer, or temperature-regulated skillet is not available, frying temperature may be estimated by dropping a bread cube into the hot fat. When the temperature is correct, the bread will be delicately browned within one minute.

Cook only a few doughnuts at one time for the best results. Too many doughnuts in the pan will lower the temperature and cause a greater amount of fat to be absorbed. Overcrowding will also distort the shape of the products where they touch and makes turning considerably more difficult.

ing, the doughnuts can be split, toasted, and buttered. The doughnut halves may be topped with jelly and broiled till the jam is hot and bubbly. (See also *Bread*.)

Cake Doughnuts

Delight your family and friends with warm doughnuts smelling of sweet sugar and cinnamon—

3¼ cups sifted all-purpose flour
2 teaspoons baking powder
½ teaspoon ground cinnamon
¼ teaspoon ground nutmeg
  Dash salt
2 eggs
⅔ cup sugar
1 teaspoon vanilla
⅔ cup cream
¼ cup butter or margarine, melted
½ cup sugar
½ teaspoon ground cinnamon

Sift together all-purpose flour, baking powder, ½ teaspoon ground cinnamon, the ground nutmeg, and salt. Beat eggs, ⅔ cup sugar, and the vanilla till thick and lemon-colored. Combine cream and butter; add alternately to egg mixture with flour mixture, beating till just blended after each addition. Cover and chill dough in the refrigerator about 2 hours.

Roll dough ⅜ inch thick on lightly floured surface. Cut out doughnuts with floured 2½-inch doughnut cutter. Fry in deep hot fat (375°) till golden brown, turning once (about 1 minute per side). Drain. While warm, shake in mixture of ½ cup sugar and ½ teaspoon ground cinnamon. Makes about 20 doughnuts.

Jiffy Doughnuts

In a hurry? Pop open a tube of refrigerated biscuits to make a quick and easy doughnut treat—

Stretch and slightly flatten with palm of hand each biscuit from 1 tube refrigerated biscuits (10 biscuits). With finger, punch hole in center of biscuit and shape into doughnut. Fry in deep hot fat (375°) about 2 minutes; turn once. Drain cooked doughnuts on paper toweling. Roll in mixture of ground cinnamon and sugar. Serve warm. Makes 10 doughnuts.

Apricot jam bubbles atop Apricot Split-Ups. Sprinkle broken nuts over doughnut halves and serve with steaming coffee.

Apricot Split-Ups

Cut plain doughnuts in half. Broil cut side down 3 to 4 inches from heat ½ to 1 minute. Spread cut surface with apricot jam; sprinkle with broken nuts. Broil till jam is bubbly.

Shaggy Mochas

2 teaspoons instant coffee powder
½ cup flaked coconut
1 cup sifted confectioners' sugar
2 tablespoons light cream *or* milk
12 plain doughnuts

In pint jars dissolve coffee powder in 2 tablespoons water; add coconut. Cover and shake until coconut is coffee color. Spread coconut on *ungreased* baking sheet; dry in 300° oven for about 25 minutes, stirring occasionally. To make icing, combine confectioners' sugar and cream. Frost tops of doughnuts and sprinkle with coffee-flavored coconut.

Coconut Cake Doughnuts

Flaked coconut makes this doughnut different—

2 eggs
½ cup sugar
¼ cup milk
2 tablespoons melted shortening
2⅓ cups sifted all-purpose flour
2 teaspoons baking powder
½ teaspoon salt
¾ cup flaked coconut
• • •
Sugar

Beat eggs with sugar till light; add milk and cooled shortening. Sift flour, baking powder, and salt together. Add dry ingredients and coconut to eggs; stir just till blended. Cover and chill mixture several hours. Roll on lightly floured surface to ½ inch thick. Cut out doughnuts with 2½-inch doughnut cutter. Fry in deep hot fat (375°) till brown; turn and brown other side (about 1 minute per side). Drain on paper toweling. While warm, shake in bag with sugar to coat. Makes 1 dozen.

Doughnut Twists

4 beaten eggs
⅔ cup sugar
⅓ cup milk
⅓ cup salad oil
3½ cups sifted all-purpose flour
3 teaspoons baking powder
¾ teaspoon salt
1 teaspoon ground cinnamon
½ teaspoon ground nutmeg
• • •
½ cup sugar
1 to 2 teaspoons ground cinnamon

Beat eggs and sugar till light; add milk and salad oil. Sift together flour, baking powder, salt, ground cinnamon, and ground nutmeg; add to egg mixture and mix well. Chill dough. On lightly floured surface, roll dough ¼ inch thick into a 12x16-inch rectangle. Cut strips ¾ inch wide and 6 inches long. Twist or form in knots. Let rest 15 minutes. Fry in deep hot fat (375°). Drain. Shake warm doughnuts in bag containing ½ cup sugar and 1 to 2 teaspoons ground cinnamon. Makes 2½ dozen.

Doughnut Balls

2 cups sifted all-purpose flour
¼ cup sugar
3 teaspoons baking powder
1 teaspoon salt
1 beaten egg
½ cup milk
¼ cup orange juice
¼ cup salad oil
1 teaspoon grated orange peel
½ cup coarsely chopped pecans
Sugar

Sift flour, ¼ cup sugar, baking powder, and salt together into mixing bowl. Combine egg, milk, orange juice, salad oil, and orange peel. Stir into dry ingredients. Add nuts. Stir to blend.

Drop by teaspoons into deep hot fat (about 360°) and fry till brown, about 3 minutes, on all sides, turning once. Drain on paper toweling. Roll in sugar. Makes about 2½ dozen.

Potato Doughnuts

3 eggs
1⅓ cups sugar
½ teaspoon vanilla
1 cup mashed potatoes, cooled*
2 tablespoons melted shortening
4 cups sifted all-purpose flour
6 teaspoons baking powder
2 teaspoons ground nutmeg
1 teaspoon salt
⅓ cup milk
Sugar

Beat eggs with 1⅓ cups sugar and vanilla till light. Add potatoes and shortening. Sift together dry ingredients; add alternately with milk to potato mixture, beating well after each addition. Chill 3 hours in the refrigerator.

Roll out half of dough at a time, keeping other half chilled. Roll on floured surface to ⅜ inch thick. Cut dough with floured 2-inch biscuit cutter; chill cut doughnuts for 15 minutes.

Fry in deep hot fat (375°) till brown, about 3 to 4 minutes, turning once; drain. Dip cooked doughnuts in sugar. Makes about 3 dozen.

*Cook 2 medium potatoes; mash potatoes with butter to make light and fluffy. Or use instant mashed potatoes and prepare potatoes according to package directions.

Raised Doughnuts

In large mixer bowl combine 2 packages active dry yeast and 2 cups flour. Heat 1 cup milk, ⅓ cup shortening, ⅓ cup sugar, and 1 teaspoon salt just till warm, stirring occasionally to melt shortening. Add to dry mixture in mixing bowl; add 2 eggs. Beat at low speed with electric mixer for ½ minute, scraping sides of bowl constantly. Beat 3 minutes at high speed. By hand, stir in 1½ to 2 cups flour to make moderately soft dough; mix the dough mixture well.

Place dough in greased bowl; turning once to grease surface. Cover and chill in the refrigerator about 3 hours or overnight. (If dough rises in refrigerator, punch down with fist.) Turn out on lightly floured surface and roll ⅓ inch thick. Cut with floured doughnut cutter. Set cut doughnuts aside and let rise till very light, about 30 to 40 minutes.

Fry in deep hot fat (375°) about 2 minutes or till browned, turning once. Drain on paper toweling. Drizzle warm doughnuts with Orange Glaze. Makes about 2 dozen.

Orange Glaze: In small mixing bowl thoroughly combine 1 teaspoon grated orange peel, 3 tablespoons orange juice, and 2 cups sifted confectioners' sugar. Mix well.

New Orleans Square Doughnuts

Dip in sugar and serve warm with coffee—

In large mixer bowl combine 1 package active dry yeast and 1½ cups flour. Heat together 1 cup milk, ¼ cup sugar, ½ cup shortening, and 1 teaspoon salt just till warm, stirring to melt shortening. Add to dry mixture in bowl; add 1 egg. Beat at low speed with electric mixer for ½ minute, scraping sides of bowl. Beat 3 minutes at high speed. By hand, stir in 1½ to 2 cups flour to make a moderately soft dough.

Turn out on lightly floured surface; knead smooth, about 8 minutes. Place in greased bowl, turning once to grease surface. Cover; let rise till double (1¼ hours). Punch down. Cover and let rest 10 minutes.

On lightly floured surface, roll out dough to 14x10-inch rectangle. Cut in 2-inch squares. Cover and let rise till light (30 to 40 minutes). Fry in deep hot fat (375°) about 3 minutes, turning once. Drain. While warm, dip in sugar, if desired. Makes about 3 dozen doughnuts.

Filled Doughnuts

      4 to 4½ cups sifted all-purpose
          flour
      2 packages active dry yeast
   1¼ cups milk
      ⅓ cup shortening
      ¼ cup sugar
      1 teaspoon salt
      2 eggs
              • • •
     18 prunes *or* 36 apricots
      ⅓ cup sugar
          Sugar

In large mixer bowl combine the yeast and *2 cups* of the flour. Heat milk, shortening, ¼ cup sugar, and salt just till warm, stirring occasionally to melt shortening. Add to dry mixture in mixing bowl; add eggs. Beat at low speed with electric mixer, scraping sides of bowl constantly. Beat 3 minutes at high speed. By hand, stir in enough remaining flour to make a soft dough.

Turn out on floured surface and knead till smooth and elastic, about 5 to 8 minutes. Place in greased bowl, turning to grease surface. Cover; let rise till double, about 45 to 60 minutes.

Meanwhile, cook fruit following package directions, adding ⅓ cup sugar at beginning of cooking. Cool; halve and pit prunes but leave apricots whole. Cut dough in half for easy handling. Roll ⅜ inch thick; cut with a 2½-inch round cutter. Place prune half or apricot in each round of dough; fold dough over fruit and seal edges. Cover and let rise in warm place till double, about 20 minutes. Fry in deep hot fat (375°) till golden, about 1 minute on each side. Drain on paper toweling. Roll in sugar. Makes about 3 dozen doughnuts.

Cinnamon Doughnuts

Taste almost like freshly baked—

     12 plain doughnuts
      ½ cup sugar
      1 to 2 teaspoons ground cinnamon

Heat doughnuts on baking sheet at 375° till very hot, about 5 minutes. Remove hot doughnuts from oven and shake in paper or plastic sack containing mixture of sugar and ground cinnamon till coated. Serve warm.

Broken nuts perch atop chocolate-dipped Rocky-Road Rings—an easy snack to be served with fresh fruit and coffee.

Orange Doughnuts

      1 package active dry yeast
      4 to 4½ cups sifted all-purpose
          flour
      1 cup orange juice
      ½ cup sugar
      ¼ cup butter
      2 teaspoons grated orange peel
      1 egg

In large mixer bowl combine yeast and *2 cups* flour. Heat orange juice, sugar, butter, orange peel, and ¾ teaspoon salt just till warm, stirring occasionally to melt butter. Add to dry mixture in mixing bowl; add egg. Beat at low speed with electric mixer for ½ minute, scraping sides of bowl constantly. Beat 3 minutes at high speed. By hand, stir in enough of the remaining flour to make soft dough.

Turn out on floured surface; knead till smooth. Place in greased bowl, turning to grease surface. Chill dough 1½ to 2 hours. Roll to ½ inch thick. Cut with floured doughnut cutter. Let rise about 1¼ hours. Fry in deep hot fat (375°). Drain. Dust with confectioners' sugar, if desired. Makes about 1½ dozen.

Rocky-Road Rings

Another time drizzle with confectioners' sugar icing and top with coconut—

      ½ cup semisweet chocolate pieces
      8 plain doughnuts
          Coarsely broken walnuts

Melt semisweet chocolate pieces over hot, not boiling, water. Dip tops of plain doughnuts in melted chocolate, then in coarsely broken walnuts. Makes 8 servings.

Crullers

Let the children twist the sweet doughnut dough into other interesting shapes—

      2 packages active dry yeast
   3¼ to 3¾ cups sifted all-purpose
          flour
          •   •   •
      1 cup milk
      ¼ cup shortening
      ⅓ cup sugar
   1½ teaspoons salt
          •   •   •
      1 egg

In large mixer bowl combine yeast and 1¾ *cups* of the flour. Heat together milk, shortening, sugar, and salt just till warm, stirring occasionally to melt shortening. Add to dry mixture in mixing bowl; add egg. Beat at low speed with electric mixer for ½ minute, scraping sides of bowl constantly. Beat 3 minutes at high speed. By hand, stir in enough of the remaining flour to make a moderately stiff dough.

Turn out on lightly floured surface; knead till smooth, about 8 minutes. Place in greased bowl, turning once to grease the surface; cover and let rise till double, about 1 to 1½ hours. Punch down. Let rest 10 minutes. On lightly floured surface roll into 12x9-inch rectangle, ½ inch thick. Cut in half crosswise; cut each half into 12 strips. Roll each strip under hands to make 10-inch strip; twist for crullers. Bring ends together. Seal ends; twist 3 times. Cover; let rise till almost double, about 45 minutes. Fry in deep hot fat (375°) about 1½ to 2 minutes, turning once; drain. Brush with a confectioners' icing, if desired. Makes 2 dozen.

DOVE—A young wild pigeon, small in size. A young dove has darker flesh and less fat than an old bird which makes the age of the dove important to its eating qualities.

Aging the bird by hanging by its feet in a cool, dry place for three to four days is important to the flavor of the dark, rich meat. Dressing procedures for a dove are the same as for domesticated birds.

Recipes used for preparing dove should suit the age and size of the bird. Recipes suitable for tame varieties of the pigeon family can be used for dove. A sophisticated and elegant meat to prepare, dove may be stuffed or braised in butter and white wine. (See also *Pigeon*.)

DRAIN—To draw off liquid from a food. Draining is usually that part of the cooking procedure which involves the gradual or complete removal of fat, water, or other liquid from another solid food.

A sieve or colander is often used to drain such foods as water from macaroni or spaghetti. A canned fruit or vegetable can be drained by pouring the liquid from the can. Excess fat is removed from deep-fat fried foods, such as doughnuts or French fried potatoes, by laying the food on paper toweling after cooking it.

DRAW—1. To eviscerate or disembowel, as when preparing poultry or fish; remove entrails. 2. To clarify butter. 3. To withdraw essence by steeping, as tea.

DRAWN BUTTER—1. Melted butter. 2. Clarified butter with seasonings added.

Drawn butter was a common ingredient listed in early day cook books. The butter was melted and mixed with hot water, flour, and seasonings. It was one way by which colonial homemakers made butter go farther. Today's classic butter sauce is also made with melted butter but with the addition of flour, seasonings, and lemon juice. Sometimes meat or fish stock is added instead of hot water to give flavor.

Drawn butter and drawn butter sauces are used with fish and meat dishes as well as with vegetables. Hot drawn butter served in individual sauce warmers enhances an elegant lobster dinner. Drizzle drawn butter sauces over other fish as well as meat dishes for rich flavor. Dress up vegetables with seasoned drawn butter sauce. (See also *Butter*.)

DREDGE—To coat or dust food with a dry ingredient. The food, such as meat or fish, can be rolled in crumbs or flour. Food pieces can be put in a paper or plastic bag with dry ingredients and shaken gently till coated completely with the mixture, as with sugar-coated doughnuts.

Dredging serves three useful purposes in connection with the cooking and palatability of food: adding flavor, facilitating browning, and improving the appearance of cooked food. Spices and seasonings may be added to the dry mixture before dredging to add additional flavor.

The dredging process also facilitates browning, such as vegetable pieces coated with flour or fish sprinkled with bread crumbs that are to be fried in fat or baked. The improved appearance of food is evidenced in the eye appeal of a crisp, golden chicken leg that has been rolled in cereal or cracker crumbs.

DRESSED—1. Poultry, fish, or game that has been cleaned and prepared for cooking. 2. Mixing a food with a seasoning or sauce before serving, such as when tossing a salad and its dressing.

Dressing procedures for meat differ from those used for fish. Fowl and poultry require plucking, drawing, trimming, and sometimes singeing. The trimming usually involves removing the head and cutting the legs off at the first joint. Singeing, or passing the bird over a flame, removes small feathers that are hard to pluck by hand. Game birds are larded to prevent drying out. This is done by tying bacon or salt pork around the bird before cooking.

Some fish need to be scaled, others skinned, and all drawn. Large game is skinned and drawn. Some birds are trussed, the legs being pulled close to the body and fastened with skewers or string, before cooking to retain the body juices.

When a salad is tossed with oil and vinegar, or vegetables are coated with melted butter before serving, they are said to be dressed. This is done to enhance the flavor of fresh or cooked food.

DRESSING — 1. A flavorful sauce-type topping, most often cold, used for salads, fruits, and meats. 2. A seasoned stuffing of a food, such as bread, rice, or potatoes, mixed with diced vegetables or fruits and used to fill the cavity of meat, poultry, or hollowed-out fruits and vegetables.

Salad dressings, most often mixtures of fats, acids, and seasonings, can be categorized into three basic types: French or basic pour dressings, basic thick mayonnaise, and cooked salad dressings.

Dressings used for stuffing usually begin with a starchy food base, such as bread, rice, or cornmeal, and then individual tastes and preferences take over with the addition of diced fruits and vegetables, zesty herbs and seasonings, and fats. A poultry or fish stuffing often serves to keep the meat moist, extend the number of servings, and retain the shape of the bird or fish during roasting period. Holiday poultry stuffings become almost as special as the bird itself. (See *Salad Dressing, Stuffing* for additional information.)

DRIED or DRYING — 1. The removal of moisture from a food as a means of food preservation. 2. Dehydration.

Spreading foods such as grapes, plums, figs, corn, and beans in the sun was man's earliest means of food preservation. Later, meat and fish were also dried. The pemmican of the American frontiersman was a mixture of dried meat and sun-dried berries sometimes mixed with fat. It was concentrated food which was easy to carry and did not need to be refrigerated.

Because modern processors can control temperature and humidity 365 days a year, few foods are dried by the idiosyncrasies of the sun's rays alone. Mechanical air circulation under carefully controlled conditions is the most frequent process, but freeze dehydration promises to be commercially important. In addition to the actual drying procedures, there are special techniques such as pasteurization which insure complete sterilization and the absence of harmful bacterial growth. Exposing the food to sulfur fumes prevents decaying and speeds the drying process.

The advantages of dried foods are: no refrigeration or special care is required before the package is opened; and being less bulky and thus easier to store, they are a concentrated form of energy.

The flavor and appearance as well as the aroma of a dried food is different from fresh food. Many dried foods such as fruit are delicious as they come from the package. Due to the concentration, color and flavor qualities are improved.

Though flavor is often concentrated, the nutritive content is sometimes altered by the drying process. Vitamin retention depends on the quality of the fresh food, the preparation of the food for drying, and the moisture-removing process. In fruits, for example, vitamin A is destroyed by prolonged sun-drying and, although sulfuring improves quality, it affects the thiamine content adversely. Ascorbic acid content varies both with the type of fruit and the drying processes applied.

There is more variation in the nutrient change in fruits than in vegetables. In vegetables the thiamine loss due to sulfuring is not serious although ascorbic acid is usually completely eliminated. Vegetables usually retain almost all of their vitamin A during the drying processes.

The principle dried vegetables include peas, beans, and lentils, and the most common dried fruits are apples, apricots, peaches, prunes, and raisins.

The same dried food advantages apply to commercial food products: 1. no refrigeration before package is opened, 2. less bulky and easier to store, and 3. concentrated energy source.

In addition to fruits and vegetables, other foods are commercially dried and include dried herbs and spices, such as dried parsley and onion flakes, thyme, celery, mint, and green pepper. Also included are dried soup mixes, dried egg, and dried milk. (See also *Dehydration*.)

DRIED BEEF — Cured top round beef that has been pickled, smoked, dried, and cut wafer-thin for packaging. Dried beef, often called chipped beef, is a preserved, salted meat distinguished by its dark red color and its concentrated smoky flavor. The pickling process, similar to that for corned beef, takes about eight weeks. The beef is then smoked for two days and subjected to a drying process for two weeks before being cut into thin slices.

Dried beef is available chipped or sliced and packaged in foil or jars. Smoked sliced beef, a different product entirely, can be distinguished from dried beef by its lighter color and less salty flavor.

When buying dried beef, check for the characteristic red beef color. The meat should be free from brown spots. The sliced, packaged meat usually has been cut in larger slices than those slices which come in small, glass jars.

Keep dried beef in refrigerator after opening. Unopened jars may be stored on the kitchen shelf up to six weeks if the room temperature is not too warm. Freezing dried beef is not recommended because undesirable flavors develop in cured meats stored at freezing temperatures.

Dried beef is packaged for use in sandwiches or as an ingredient. When used as an ingredient, some of the salty flavor can be removed by covering the meat with hot water for a minute and draining. When this is not done, little or no salt needs to be added to recipes using dried beef.

Dried beef is often served as creamed beef on toast; for variety drizzle creamed beef over baked potatoes or popovers. Or, pair it with potatoes, rice, or noodles in a casserole. Dried beef is also tasty when cooked in bacon drippings or butter and crumbled in scrambled eggs, salads, or vegetables. (See also *Beef*.)

Dried Beef Log

1 8-ounce package cream cheese, softened
¼ cup grated Parmesan cheese
1 tablespoon prepared horseradish
⅓ cup chopped pimiento-stuffed green olives
2½ ounces dried beef, finely snipped

Blend cream cheese, Parmesan cheese, and horseradish. Stir in olives. On waxed paper shape mixture in two 6-inch rolls. Wrap and chill several hours or overnight. Roll in snipped beef. Serve with crackers.

Save time and utensils by snipping several slices dried beef right into measuring cup. Separate the pieces before using in recipe.

Chipped Beef Puff

4 ounces dried beef, snipped
¼ cup butter or margarine
3 tablespoons all-purpose flour
2 cups milk
2 tablespoons chopped canned pimiento
1 3-ounce can sliced mushrooms, drained (½ cup)
Cheese Topper

Cook dried beef in butter or margarine over low heat, stirring till slightly crisp and frizzled. Blend in flour and dash pepper. Stir in milk all at once; cook and stir till mixture thickens and bubbles. Stir in pimiento and drained mushrooms. Pour into 10x6x1¾-inch baking dish. Keep dried beef mixture hot in 375° oven while making the cheese topper.

Cheese Topper: Beat 3 egg whites with ¼ teaspoon salt till stiff peaks form. Beat 3 egg yolks till thick and lemon-colored. Fold yolks into whites; fold in ⅓ cup shredded process American cheese. Pour over hot beef mixture. Bake at 375° till golden brown, about 15 to 20 minutes. Garnish with additional frizzled dried beef. Makes 4 or 5 servings.

Beef and Noodle Bake

Rinse 3 ounces, snipped (1 cup), dried beef with hot water; drain. In saucepan melt 2 tablespoons butter; blend in 2 tablespoons all-purpose flour, ½ teaspoon salt, and ¼ teaspoon pepper. Stir in 1½ cups milk. Cook and stir till mixture thickens and bubbles. Mix in dried beef; 1 teaspoon prepared mustard; ¼ cup chopped celery; 2 tablespoons chopped green pepper, 2 hard-cooked eggs, chopped; and 2 ounces (1 cup) medium noodles, cooked.

Turn into 1-quart casserole, or divide between four 8-ounce individual casseroles. Mix 1 cup soft bread crumbs with 2 tablespoons melted butter; sprinkle atop.

Bake at 350° for 15 to 20 minutes for individual casseroles or 30 to 35 minutes for 1-quart casserole. Makes 4 servings.

Creamed Dried Beef

      4 ounces dried or smoked dried
          beef*, torn
      2 tablespoons butter
      2 tablespoons all-purpose flour
      1 cup milk
            • • •
      ½ teaspoon Worcestershire sauce
          Toast points

Cook dried beef in butter till edges frizzle. Push meat to one side; blend flour into butter. Stir in milk all at once. Cook, stirring constantly, till thick and bubbly, gradually incorporating dried beef. Add Worcestershire and dash pepper. Spoon over buttered toast. Serves 3.

*If dried beef is extra salty, let stand a few minutes in boiling water. Drain on paper toweling before cooking in the butter.

DRIED FRUIT—Ripe fruit that has been processed by sun-drying or mechanical-drying techniques. Dried fruits were eaten by everyday people before the Christian Era, being used extensively by the Egyptians. Before the twentieth century, dried fruits were imported to the United States.

How dried fruit is produced: Most dried fruit found in the markets today is processed in this country either by sun-drying or mechanical-drying techniques with the former being traditional and the latter the most convenient method.

The sun-dried fruits usually dry two to three weeks after ripening. Sulfuring (exposing the fruits to sulfur fumes) ensures color retention, serves as an insect repellent, prevents decaying, speeds drying, and influences vitamin retention.

Mechanical-drying techniques use artificial heat and often natural or forced air ventilation. Sulfuring is also part of the mechanical-drying method.

Fruits are dried in different ways depending on the particular fruit. Prunes, figs, and raisins are dried whole, while apples are peeled, cored, and sliced before drying processes. Ripe figs drop from the tree already partially dried.

Inspection and grading of dried fruits ensure uniform packaging. Good packaging is very important in maintaining the moist quality of the firm, meaty fruit.

Nutritional value: Although over 50 percent of the water is evaporated, many of the nutrients still remain after the drying process. Vitamin A is sometimes altered by extensive sun-drying periods, while ascorbic acid loss varies with the fruit as well as with the drying treatment.

If the dried fruit is eaten as purchased, the caloric value extends to four or five times that of the same fresh fruit. A pound and a half of dried fruits equals the mineral equivalent of six to eight pounds fresh fruit. All dried fruits are a good source of energy because of the simple fruit sugar which the body naturally assimilates. This fruit sugar requires no digestive action. Prunes and raisins are good iron suppliers. Apricots are rich in vitamins A and C.

How to select: Most dried fruits are available in sealed cartons or bags throughout the year. All dried fruits are graded and grouped according to their size. Five grades have been set up and are indicated on the package of dried fruit. The five grades are Extra Fancy, Fancy, Extra Choice, Choice, and Standard.

A label indicating that the fruit is "tenderized" means a shorter cooking period is required. Fruit is packaged according to

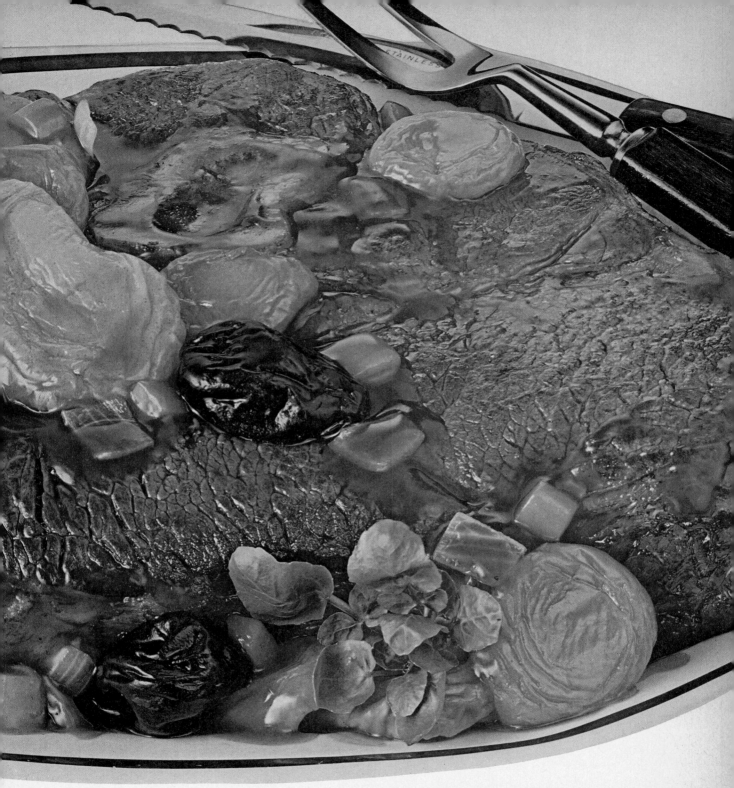

Add main dish color to the meal by combining dried fruit and tasty cider mixture to make mouth-watering Fruited Pot Roast.

individual type or in assorted mixtures suitable for use in recipes requiring combinations of fruits. Packaged dried fruit should be free of dirt, mold, insects, other foreign matter, and musty odor.

How to store: The concentrated simple sugars of dried fruit serve as a natural preservative, so caring for and storing the fruit is relatively simple. Vacuum-packed in cartons or transparent film bags, the fruit will keep up to six or eight months on the kitchen shelf or in the refrigerator.

Store leftover fruit from an opened package in a tightly covered container in a cool, dry place. Dried fruits need to be stored in the refrigerator during hot weather months to retain fruit quality.

How To Cook Dried Fruit

Rinse fruit and cover with water 1 inch above fruit in saucepan. Cover; simmer gently for time specified in chart. If desired, add sugar last 5 minutes of cooking.

To plump raisins, cover with water in saucepan. Bring to boiling. Remove from heat; let stand, covered, 5 minutes.

Dried fruit	Cooking time in minutes*	Sugar**
Apples	20 to 30	4
Apricots	20 to 25	3 to 4
Figs	40 to 45	1
Mixed Fruits	25 to 30	2 to 3
Peaches	30 to 35	3 to 4
Pears	30 to 35	3 to 4
Prunes	10 to 20	2

*Some dried fruits are processed to cut cooking time. See cooking directions on package.

**Sugar in tablespoons per cup uncooked fruit.

How to prepare: Formerly, drying techniques left fruits hard and withered, requiring tedious long soaking and cooking periods. Today, dried fruits require little or no soaking, and quick cooking is necessary to retain the delicate fruit pulps.

Oversoaking produces a watery, tasteless fruit. Hot water hastens soaking and leaves the fruit plumper than does cold water. Fruit should not be crowded in water so it has a chance to rehydrate and properly cook. Add sugar, if extra sweetness is desired, during the last five minutes of cooking as sugar inhibits the absorption of water. Fruits may be baked for dessert in the oven right along with other foods for a meal. The fruits will come out juicy and plump and will not require any additional preparation before serving.

Different dried fruits take up varying amounts of water during cooking. Apricots, figs, prunes, and raisins double in bulk by the end of cooking period. Peaches and pears triple in bulk and apples increase in bulk by five times.

The amount of fresh fruit needed to produce one pound of each type dried fruit helps explain the differing size increases of the cooked fruit. To make one pound of each fruit it takes seven to ten pounds of apples, six to seven pounds of peaches, six to seven pounds of pears, two and one half to three pounds of plums for prunes, and four pounds of grapes for raisins.

How to use: Dried fruits are delicious energy-givers eaten right out of the carton or bag. Make fruit purées by cooking fruits longer with added water and putting through sieve. Cook favorite dried fruit and serve as a sauce with dessert topping or as a meat accompaniment.

Add delectable flavors to pies, cakes, and cookies with chopped, cooked fruits. Bread puddings and stuffings for meat and fish acquire tasty flavor and new texture when dried fruits are added.

Colorful dried fruits make delightful meal garnishes and a wide assortment of tasty appetizers. Single fruits or assorted fruit mixtures are suitable for use in a simple compote or cold fruit soup served for wintertime desserts and snacks or at brunches. (See also *Fruit*.)

Fruited Pot Roast

Colorful meat accompaniment adds new flavor—

    12 dried apricots
    12 dried prunes
     1 3- to 4-pound beef chuck
          pot roast
     1 cup cider *or* apple juice
     2 tablespoons sugar
    ¼ teaspoon ground cinnamon
    ¼ teaspoon ground ginger
     3 whole cloves
    1½ cups sliced onions

Cover apricots and prunes with water. Soak several hours. Meanwhile, brown pot roast on both sides in a little hot fat; season with salt and pepper. Combine cider, sugar, cinnamon, ginger, and cloves; pour over meat. Add onions. Cover; simmer till meat is almost tender, about 2 hours. Drain fruits; place atop meat and cook 30 minutes longer. Thicken liquid in pan for gravy. Makes 6 to 8 servings.

Fruit Compote Pie

Fruit flavors blend in a refreshing dessert pie—

     1 cup mixed dried fruits, cut
          in pieces
    ½ cup orange juice
    ¼ cup raisins
    ¼ cup sugar
     1 tablespoon quick-cooking
          tapioca
     1 baked 9-inch pastry shell
             •   •   •
     1 3-ounce package no-bake
          custard mix
     2 cups milk
    ½ teaspoon shredded orange peel

In medium saucepan combine dried fruits, orange juice, ½ cup water, raisins, sugar, and tapioca; let stand 5 minues. Bring to full rolling boil; reduce heat and simmer till fruits are tender, about 10 minutes, stirring frequently. Cool; turn into baked pastry shell. Combine custard mix and milk; cook and cool according to package directions for custard pie. Pour carefully over fruit layer. Sprinkle with orange peel. Chill 3 to 4 hours before serving.

Fruit Confections

     1 cup raisins
    ¾ cup dried apricots
    ½ cup pitted dates
     1 cup walnuts
     2 tablespoons honey
             •   •   •
     2 tablespoons sugar
    ½ teaspoon ground cinnamon

Grind fruits and nuts with coarse blade of a food grinder. Mix with honey. Shape into 1-inch balls. Combine sugar and cinnamon. Roll balls in sugar mixture *or* sifted confectioners' sugar, if desired. Makes about 3 dozen 1-inch balls.

Fruit Balls

    1½ cups prunes, cooked and
          pitted
    1½ cups pitted dates
    ¾ cup dried apricots
    ½ cup raisins
     1 cup walnuts
    ¼ cup sugar
    ¼ cup orange juice concentrate,
          thawed
     1 3½-ounce can flaked
          coconut (1⅓ cups)

Grind prunes, dates, apricots, raisins, and walnuts with coarse blade of a food grinder. Add sugar and orange juice. Form into 1-inch balls; roll in coconut. Makes 10 dozen.

Harvest Fruit Compote

     1 16-ounce package dried prunes
    ½ of 11-ounce package dried
          apricots (1⅓ cups)
     1 13½-ounce can pineapple
          chunks, undrained (1⅔ cups)
             •   •   •
     1 21-ounce can cherry pie filling
     2 cups water
    ¼ cup dry sherry

In 9x2-inch baking dish, layer prunes, apricots, and pineapple. Combine remaining ingredients; pour over fruit. Cover and bake at 350° for 1½ hours. Serve warm. Serves 8.

DROP—1. A minute quantity of liquid that falls in a single globule. 2. A soft batter or dough shaped with a spoon into biscuits, cookies, or dumplings.

Liquid flavorings, such as peppermint or lemon, are often measured in number of drops or degree of flow as "drop by drop." An eye-dropper is used when the exact number of drops is vitally important.

Batter or dough of drop consistency, as in biscuits or cookies, indicates the liquid proportion is high and, therefore, makes it unlikely that the product can be shaped with the hands. A spoon is most frequently used for shaping and then the food is dropped directly from the spoon onto baking sheet or stew, or pushed off the spoon with the aid of another spoon.

DROP BISCUIT—Biscuit baked from standard biscuit dough to which more liquid has been added. The same basic flour, shortening, and milk ingredients are leavened with baking powder or baking soda as for standard biscuits. The added liquid gives the biscuit a softer consistency and a spoon is needed to shape it.

Biscuits can be dropped by rounded spoonfuls onto a greased baking sheet or into muffin cups. If biscuits are dropped close together, they will bake together and have soft sides. Baking biscuits farther apart or in the muffin cups will produce crisp, tender sides. Baked drop biscuits will have a somewhat pebbly browned top as compared to the smooth top of a standard biscuit. (See also *Biscuit.*)

Drop Biscuits

    2 cups sifted all-purpose flour
    3 teaspoons baking powder
    ½ teaspoon salt
    ¼ cup shortening
    1 cup milk

Sift dry ingredients together into bowl. Cut in shortening with pastry blender or two forks till mixture looks like coarse crumbs. Make a well; add milk all at once. Stir quickly with fork till ingredients are moistened. Drop from teaspoon onto greased baking sheet. Bake at 450° for 12 to 15 minutes. Makes 16 biscuits.

DROP COOKIE—A soft-dough cookie shaped by dropping the dough from a spoon onto a baking sheet. One of the quickest and easiest types of cookies to make, drop cookies are acceptable in dainty sizes or as big, round sugar cookies.

A variety of shapes and forms can be achieved with drop cookie dough. If the dough is not lumpy, force some batters through a pastry bag. The dough is softer than a rolled cookie, yet stiff enough to be shaped and molded into balls or swirled shapes. Flatten some drop cookies with a glass that has been dipped in sugar, or make a crisscross pattern with a fork. Decorate drop cookies using raisins, assorted candies, and coconut. Stir candied fruits, nuts, or raisins into others.

Space drop cookies at regular intervals on the cookie sheet so they will not bake into each other and will bake evenly. Chill and mound the cookie dough before baking to prevent the cookie from spreading. Using a cool cookie sheet for each baking also eliminates spreading. Move cookies from cookie sheet to cooling rack immediately, as they continue to bake on sheet.

Drop cookies store well. Maintain moist qualities of the cookie by keeping them in a covered container. The drop cookie packs well and makes an excellent gift for mailing. (See also *Cookie.*)

Problems with drop cookies?

A doughy texture indicates that the cookie has not been baked long enough. A dry-textured cookie with dark brown edges means the cookie has been baked too long.

Brown-Eyed Susan Cookies

Combine 1½ cups packaged biscuit mix, two 3¾- or 3⅝-ounce packages *instant* vanilla pudding mix, ⅓ cup salad oil, and 2 eggs; mix well. Drop cookies from teaspoon onto *ungreased* cookie sheet. Flatten each cookie slightly. Top each with 6 or 7 mint-flavored chocolate pieces. Bake at 350° for 12 to 14 minutes. Spread melted chocolate over tops. Makes about 42.

Drop cookies are dropped from spoon or aided by another spoon or spatula onto greased baking sheet. Space cookies evenly apart.

Treat the family to spicy-rich Oatmeal Cookies. The pebbly topped, plump cookies are chock full of raisins and chopped nuts.

Oatmeal Cookies

> 1 cup shortening
> 1½ cups brown sugar
> 2 eggs
> ½ cup buttermilk or sour milk*
> 1¾ cups sifted all-purpose flour
> 1 teaspoon baking soda*
> 1 teaspoon baking powder*
> 1 teaspoon ground cinnamon
> 1 teaspoon ground nutmeg
> 3 cups quick-cooking rolled oats
> 1 cup raisins
> ½ cup chopped walnuts

Cream shortening, sugar, and eggs till light. Stir in buttermilk. Sift together dry ingredients and 1 teaspoon salt; stir into creamed mixture. Stir in oats, raisins, and nuts. Drop from tablespoon 2 inches apart on lightly greased cookie sheet. Bake at 400° about 8 minutes. Cool slightly; remove. Makes 60.

   *Or use sweet milk; reduce baking soda to ¼ teaspoon and use 2 teaspoons baking powder.

Butter Pecan Cookies

> 1 cup butter or margarine
> ¾ cup brown sugar
> ¾ cup granulated sugar
> 2 eggs
> 1 teaspoon vanilla
> 2¼ cups sifted all-purpose flour
> 1 teaspoon baking soda
> 1 cup chopped pecans

Cream butter and sugars till light. Beat in eggs and vanilla. Sift together flour, soda, and ½ teaspoon salt; blend into creamed mixture. Stir in nuts. Drop from teaspoon on *ungreased* cookie sheet. Bake at 375° about 10 minutes. Makes about 4 dozen cookies.

Funny-Face Cookies

½ cup shortening
1 cup brown sugar
½ cup light molasses
½ cup milk
2 teaspoons vinegar
2½ cups sifted all-purpose flour
½ teaspoon baking soda
½ teaspoon salt
½ teaspoon ground ginger
½ teaspoon ground cinnamon
Wooden skewers
Raisins, assorted candies,
coconut
Corn syrup

Cream together shortening, brown sugar, and molasses. Stir in milk and vinegar. Sift together flour, soda, salt, ginger, and cinnamon; stir into molasses mixture. Drop by tablespoon about 2½ inches apart on lightly greased cookie sheet. Insert wooden skewer halfway into cookie dough mound. Stagger rows of cookies to leave room for the skewers. Use small spatula to spread dough around skewer if dough separates. Bake at 350° for 15 to 20 minutes. Decorate faces with raisins, candies, and coconut. Brush decorations with corn syrup to secure. Let stand before removing to rack.

DRY MILK — Whole or skim milk from which the water has been removed.

This convenient dairy product is produced and marketed in three forms: nonfat dry milk, instant nonfat dry milk, and dry whole milk. For each dry milk form, the manufacturing process is basically the same; only the products differ.

Nonfat dry milk: This starts out as fresh whole milk. The first step is the removal of milk fat from the fresh milk. The remaining nonfat portion is then put through a pasteurization process in which a large portion of the moisture is evaporated. Sprayed into a drying chamber, the milk is exposed to heated air filters which evaporate the remaining moisture and form the dry, white particles called dry milk.

The nutritional value of dry milk is not altered by these processes. In fact, the fat removal for the nonfat milk makes this milk form even more desirable for special diets and for weight watchers. The milk solids of lactose, milk protein, and minerals are readily available in dry milk.

Instant nonfat dry milk: This is the most popular of the three forms and can easily be found in supermarkets. Dry milk is instantized by moistening it, causing the dry milk particles to clump together, and then redrying. Instant nonfat dry milk is available in packages or jars. Buy the size to fit family and cooking needs.

Dry whole milk: Although this form is not often found in the United States, when it is, it is often used for infant feeding.

After milk has been reconstituted with water, it should be refrigerated in a manner similar to fresh milk. Dried whole milk, requiring special packaging because of the milk fat content, does not store easily.

Nonfat dry milk is used commercially in such foods as prepared mixes, bakery products, dairy foods, baby foods, and others. Use dry milk at home in place of fresh milk. Reconstitute milk according to package directions and add to recipe or add dry milk to dry ingredients and then add liquid. Use dry milk in desserts and toppings. Added to meat mixtures, dry milk holds in juices. (See also *Milk*.)

DRY WINE — A red or white unsweetened wine brought about by the fermentation of all of the sugar into alcohol. This results in the dry taste. Dry wines are perishable and should be consumed within 48 hours after opening. Dry wines are often served as appetizer or table wines when entertaining guests. (See also *Wines and Spirits*.)

DUCHESS POTATO — Mashed or puréed potatoes mixed with egg yolks and butter having salt, pepper, and sometimes nutmeg added. The fluffy, light potatoes, de-

Mashed potato elegance

Transform ordinary potatoes into a special→ surprise by mixing mashed potatoes, egg, and seasonings. Bake the Duchess Potatoes.

veloped by the French, can be shaped into many forms. Duchess potatoes may be forced through a pastry tube to pipe the edges of a steak or used as a fish or meat garnish. Decorate a casserole with potato rosettes. Pipe the potatoes onto a baking sheet, making individual servings; then broil them until they are done.

Duchess potatoes are often used as a beginning step for other potato and main dish recipes. Shaped potato croquettes are rolled in bread crumbs and deep fried. Serve creamed dishes in individual potato cases. Sometimes the potatoes are used as filling for stuffed baked potatoes or twice-baked potatoes. Glaze small portions of duchess potatoes and bake in oven to serve with a company meal instead of baked potatoes, which are the usual starch item at such affairs. (See also *Potato*.)

Duchess Potatoes

2 cups hot mashed potatoes
1 tablespoon butter or margarine
1 beaten egg yolk
  Salt
  Pepper
1 tablespoon butter or margarine, melted

To potatoes add 1 tablespoon butter or margarine, the egg yolk, and salt and pepper to taste; mix well. Push mounds from spoon onto greased baking sheet. Drizzle with remaining 1 tablespoon melted butter or margarine. Bake at 450° 10 to 12 minutes. Serves 4 to 6.

DUCK AND DUCKLING—Wild or domestic bird sought for its dark meat and distinctive flavor. Duck refers to the older duck, over eight weeks, and more specifically to the female bird. The male bird is called the drake. Duckling designates the young bird of less than eight weeks old. Both terms are used in the United States, but duckling is more correct as most birds sold in the United States are young.

The web-footed bird makes its home near fresh water. Various types of ducks exhibit different plumage colorings, but the basic down and feather covering is the same for all ducks. The soft down coat situated underneath the plumage protects the bird from cold weather. This soft down is often used for pillow filling. The duck uses an oil gland located at the base of the tail to keep the outer thick plumage groomed and cleaned at all times.

The birds' diets range from fish to grass and seeds, depending on the kind of bird and the water environment. The flavor of its meat is greatly affected by the diet of the bird as well as by its age and weight.

Ducks have been hunted as a major source of food since the earliest days of recorded time. The hieroglyphics of the ancient Egyptians show ducks being salted and dried for future use. The first people to actually breed and raise the ducks for food were the Chinese.

Domesticated ducks began to appear in Europe during the first century of the Christian Era. Romans fed figs to the ducks and then cooked them in delectable wine sauces. Ducks were an important meat source to the colonial Americans. They stored and cured the ducks in cellars, and sometimes canned them.

Types and kinds: There are over a hundred species of wild ducks found all over the world. One of the most widely known and delicately flavored is the canvasback. Getting its name from plumage coloring and a canvas bag shipment method of some years ago, the canvasback is regarded as the ultimate of wild duck dinners. The delightful, delicate flavor of the bird is contributed to by celery grass which the canvasback seeks out and thrives on.

The teal, including the green-winged, blue-winged, and cinnamon varieties, is another well-known freshwater duck. The loud whistling widgeon is a third freshwater duck known to most hunters.

The most beautiful of American ducks is the freshwater wood duck, or summer

A festive duck dinner

Carve tender duckling meat slices right at →
the table and pass tangy cranberry sauce.
Guests will enjoy Cranberry Ducklings.

duck as it is sometimes called. The wood duck flies in noiseless, graceful motion. The duck is easily domesticated and it is bred on the Pacific Coast. Freshwater ducks, unlike saltwater ducks, prefer shallow, fresh waters where little diving is required to pick up fish and other edible substances from the pond bottom.

The mallard, found in all parts of the world, is probably one of the most important ducks as far as abundance and flavor are concerned. Being a river and pond duck, the mallard's diet consists of grains and small animal life. Many domestic varieties are descendants of the mallard.

The merganser ducks, with slender, cylindrical bills, dive for and feed on fish. The flavor of their meat is affected by this fish diet. Eight to ten types of merganser ducks, including the hooded merganser and red-breasted merganser in America, are found throughout the world.

In addition to the large number of wild ducks, commercially raised ducklings are also available. The largest percentage of commercially raised ducklings are descendants of the white Pekin duck brought from China in 1873. The white Pekin duck is a member of the mallard family.

Over one-half of the ducklings sold in America are raised on Long Island. The five million or so ducklings raised yearly in America become fine table delicacies, particularly during the holiday season.

The duckling that is raised commercially receives regulated special diets and is exposed to healthy environmental conditions in order to produce a bird with sweet, tender breast meat. The scientifically bred ducklings are not often raised during the cold months because of the difficulties encountered. Spring and summer surplus is consumed during this time.

The birds are completely dressed and cleaned for the commercial market. Bound in tight, shape-conforming plastic wrap, they are quick-frozen and ready to cook after thawing is complete.

Nutritional value: Duckling is an extremely nutritious meat to serve to the family. The dark meat is rich in protein, thiamine, and riboflavin, and is a fair source of iron. A higher fat content is found in ducklings than is present in other poultry. The soft duckling fat is highly concentrated with unsaturated fatty acids.

How to select: When buying fresh duckling, remember that most of the sliceable meat comes from the breast, so select a well-developed, broad-breasted bird. A duckling is longer in appearance than a chicken and should be adequately covered with flesh. Check the skin making sure it is free from pinfeathers, breaks in skin, and bruises.

Packaged, ready-to-cook duckling is available in weights from three and one half to five pounds. Ready-to-cook wild duck is available in one to two pound weights. Check to see that the bird has been well wrapped and that there are no breaks in the package.

Allow three-fourths to one pound of duckling meat for each person. One average-size duckling will usually serve about three persons with hearty appetites.

How to store: Keep fresh duckling in a loosely covered container in the coldest part of the refrigerator. It may be kept this way between two and three days before cooking. Leftover, cooked duckling should be refrigerated immediately where it will keep well one to two days. Ducklings freeze well and can be stored in the freezer up to three months before thawing and using.

How to prepare: To develop the rich, wild duck flavor, many hunters choose to age ducks by hanging the birds by their feet in a cool, shady place for about three days. Avid duck lovers claim that aging breaks tough meat fibers, and leaving the entrails intact during aging enhances the flavor still further. If the bird has been bruised badly, the entrails should be removed before hanging the duck to age. Otherwise, there is danger that the duck will spoil.

Dressing and cleaning fresh duck requires skill and patience. Dry picking is recommended over the hot water dunking treatment as water washes away the flavor. After removing all the outer coarse guard feathers, pour melted paraffin over the soft down and pull off when dry, being careful not to tear the skin. The entrails are then drawn and the duck singed. The tedious job of removing the pinfeathers requires a great deal of patience, and a perfectionist will usually try to remove each one with a pair of tweezers.

Cut away excess fat around body openings as there is sufficient fat on the duck to self-baste the bird. Consequently, no added fat will be needed when cooking the wild duck. Sometimes the wing tips are also clipped away for added convenience.

Opinions regarding the preparation of duck before cooking also differ. The noted duck lover will simply wipe the bird and body cavity with a damp cloth assuming the cooking process will take care of any bacterial action. The novice homemaker will soak the bird for hours in water and soda solution to rid the bird of the wild flavor. Blood retains the delicate duck flavor, so personal preference dictates which method of preparation to use.

Ducks and ducklings are often marinated in wine sauces and mixtures before cooking. Unless suitable flavorings and sauces are used, marinating sometimes destroys or covers up the rich game flavor that many people expect from wild birds.

Truss the birds with skewers or twine to hold in the body juices during cooking. Pricking the skin allows the fat juices to slowly escape and baste the bird during roasting. A roasted wild duck may need to be basted occasionally.

There are three separate thoughts on the way the duckling should be cooked. One way is to fast-cook the bird in a hot oven not over 30 minutes. This usually produces a rare, pink meat with a crisp, brown crust. A second method is to allow the bird to cook in a hot oven about five to six minutes and then reduce the temperature. The third way is to cook the bird in a

moderate oven till done. The bird may be brushed with a fruit glaze before done.

The famous French pressed duck (canard) or duckling (caneton) utilizes a special duck press apparatus, but this may be achieved at home by putting the meat through a food grinder using a coarse blade. Duck can also be roasted on the outdoor grill for a special company meal or for a special-occasion dinner-for-two.

Whatever way the bird is prepared, it should be served immediately. Avoid using strong, competitive flavors. Orange sauces or stuffings are good flavor accompaniments to duck and duckling. Any fruits, such as cherries or peaches, make colorful garnishes. (See also *Poultry*.)

Cranberry Duckling

      2 3- to 5-pound ready-to-cook
         domestic ducklings
         Giblets and neck
      1 10½-ounce can condensed beef
         broth
                • • •
      ¾ cup cranberry juice cocktail
      2 tablespoons butter or margarine
      2 tablespoons sugar
      2 tablespoons vinegar
      1 tablespoon cornstarch
      1 tablespoon cranberry juice
         cocktail

Follow directions for roasting domestic duck (see chart, page 812). Meanwhile, place neck and giblets in saucepan. Add beef broth and simmer, covered, for 1 hour. Strain broth; serve giblets with duck. To the strained broth add ¾ cup cranberry juice cocktail; cook till reduced to one cup. In small saucepan melt butter or margarine; blend in sugar; cook and stir till brown. Add the 2 tablespoons vinegar and the cranberry-broth mixture.

Remove ducklings from roasting pan to warm serving platter. Skim fat from meat juices; add juices to cranberry-broth mixture. Blend cornstarch with the 1 tablespoon cranberry juice cocktail; stir into sauce. Cook and stir till sauce thickens and bubbles; simmer 1 to 2 minutes. Pass sauce with duckling. Garnish the duckling with parsley and kumquats or other garnishes, if desired. Makes about 8 servings.

Preparing wild duck

Because of their diets, some wild ducks have a definite fish flavor. To eliminate this flavor, place celery, carrots, or potatoes in body cavity. Simmer duck in water about 10 minutes. Discard stuffing and prepare duck for roasting as usual.

Wild Duck À La Orange

A succulent duck, glistening with orange glaze,
spices the dinner-time meal—

> 2 1- to 2-pound ready-to-cook wild
> ducks, split in halves
> lengthwise
> • • •
> 1 medium onion, sliced and
> separated into rings
> 2 tablespoons butter or margarine
> • • •
> 2 tablespoons frozen orange juice
> concentrate, thawed
> 2 tablespoons honey
> 1 tablespoon lemon juice
> ½ teaspoon ground ginger
> ¼ teaspoon ground allspice

Roast duck on rack in shallow roasting pan at 400° till tender, about 1 hour. If necessary, cap with foil to prevent excess browning. Skim off fat. Last 5 to 10 minutes baste the duck with orange glaze. Makes about 4 servings.

To make orange glaze cook onion in butter till tender but not brown. Stir in thawed orange juice concentrate, honey, lemon juice, ground ginger, and ground allspice. Heat just to boiling.

Rotisserie Duck

Roast a golden duck on the barbecue grill for a
change-of-pace outdoor meal—

> 1 4-pound ready-to-cook domestic
> duckling
> • • •
> Salt
> 2 tablespoons sugar
> Pepper

Rub inside the duckling with salt. Prick skin and truss well. Balance duckling on spit, securing with holding forks on both ends. Arrange hot coals at back and sides of firebox. Place a foil drip pan in front of coals and under the spit. (Since ducks are fat birds, a large amount of fat will cook out and drip into foil pan. It may be necessary to drain fat occasionally from the drip pan so that the fat will not become too hot and flame up.)

Attach spit, turn on motor and lower the barbecue hood. Let duck rotate over *medium* coals till done, about 2 hours. (Maintain a temperature of 300° to 325° if the grill has a heat indicator.) The last 10 minutes of roasting time sprinkle the duck with sugar and dash pepper. Continue roasting till brown. Makes 4 servings.

ROASTING CHART FOR DUCK

General Instructions: Salt inside of ready-to-cook bird. Stuff as desired. Truss bird; place, breast side up, on rack on shallow roasting pan. Roast, uncovered, till tender (refer to chart). Times may vary with age of bird; young birds are the most suitable for roasting. When necessary, place foil loosely over top of bird to prevent excess browning.

Game Bird	Ready-to-Cook Weight	Oven Temp.	Roasting Time	Amount of Serving	Special Instructions
Wild Duck	1-2 lbs.	400°	60-90 min.	1-1½ lbs.	Stuff loosely with quartered onions and apples; discard stuffing before serving. Do not brush with oil.
Domestic Duckling	3-5 lbs.	375° then 425°	1½-2 hrs. 15 min.	¾-1 lb.	Prick skin well all over to allow fat to escape. Do not rub with oil. Serve stuffing with bird.

Roast Duckling with Oranges

       2 4- to 5-pound ready-to-cook
          domestic ducklings
       3 medium oranges
       2 tablespoons sugar
       2 teaspoons vinegar
       2 cups canned condensed beef
          broth
    1½ tablespoons lemon juice
       3 teaspoons cornstarch
      ½ cup sweet sherry
      ⅓ cup orange liqueur

Clean ducklings and pat dry. Rub inside of ducks with salt; skewer opening and lace shut. Prick skin well all over to allow fat to escape. Roast on a rack in shallow pan at 400°, following directions for roasting domestic duck (see chart, page 812). Spoon off fat occasionally. While ducks roast, shave peel from 2 of the oranges with vegetable parer and cut in julienne strips; squeeze the juice from *all* 3 oranges. Set orange peel and juice aside until needed.

When ducks are done, place on heated platter and keep hot while making orange sauce. To prepare sauce remove drippings from roasting pan and skim off fat; set pan juices aside. Caramelize the sugar with vinegar in roasting pan; add reserved pan juices, beef broth, orange juice and peel, and lemon juice. Cook sauce rapidly to reduce by *half*. Blend cornstarch and sherry; gradually stir into sauce. Cook and stir till thickened and clear. Add orange liqueur to the sauce just before serving. Trim ducks with several orange sections, if desired. Makes 6 to 8 servings.

Roast Domestic Duck

Fruit- or celery-stuffed duck is a company treat—

Remove wing tips and first juice from one 3- to 5-pound ready-to-cook domestic duck. Sprinkle inside with salt. Stuff lightly with Orange Stuffing (see *Stuffing* for recipe), *or* celery and 1 quartered, tart apple. Prick skin all over to allow fat to escape. Do not rub with oil. Truss; place breast up on rack in shallow pan. Don't add water. Roast, uncovered, at 375° for 1½ to 2 hours. Increase temperature to 425° and cook until leg moves quite easily when tested, about 15 minutes. Makes 3 or 4 servings.

Navy Bean–Stuffed Duck

       1 cup dry small navy beans
       2 chicken bouillon cubes
      ½ pound bulk pork sausage,
          broken in bite-size pieces
       1 medium tomato, peeled and
          chopped
      ½ cup finely chopped onion
      ¼ cup finely chopped celery
      ¼ cup snipped parsley
       1 small clove garlic, minced
      ½ teaspoon dried thyme leaves,
          crushed
       1 small bay leaf
      ¼ cup sauterne
              • • •
       1 5- to 6-pound ready-to-cook
          domestic duckling

In saucepan combine beans, 1 quart water, and chicken bouillon cubes; bring to boiling and boil gently for 2 minutes. Remove from heat; cover and let stand for 1 hour.

To the bean mixture, add sausage, tomato, onion, celery, parsley, garlic, thyme, bay leaf, and ¼ teaspoon salt. Bring to boiling; cover and simmer 1 hour. Uncover and stir in wine. Boil the mixture gently, uncovered, till the liquid is absorbed, about 30 minutes.

Salt inside of duckling; stuff lightly and truss. Roast, following directions for roasting domestic duck (see chart, page 824). Makes 4 servings.

Cantonese Duck

Season two 1- to 2-pound ready-to-cook wild ducks inside and out with salt. Place in cavity of *each* bird ½ orange, cut in wedges, and a few celery leaves. Place birds, breast side up, on rack in a shallow roasting pan. Roast, uncovered, at 400° till tender, about 1 hour. If necessary, cap with foil to prevent excess browning.

Meanwhile, prepare sauce by combining ½ cup apricot preserves, ¼ cup water, 1 tablespoon prepared mustard, 1 tablespoon soy sauce, 1 tablespoon lemon juice, and ½ teaspoon monosodium glutamate in a saucepan. Heat, stirring constantly. During the last 10 minutes of roasting, baste ducks occasionally with sauce. Remove meat from oven; discard stuffing. Serve ducks over hot cooked rice; pass remaining sauce. Makes 4 servings.

DUCK PRESS—Equipment used to press duck for particular duck dishes prepared at the table. The aluminum and stainless steel apparatus consists of a container which holds the meat and a press which forces the juices from the meat.

The duck is roasted without stuffing to a rare stage. The breast is sliced into fillets and the legs are removed. The remainder of the carcass is put through the duck press along with red wine, and the extracted juices are served as gravy or sauce with the breast and leg meat.

The French extract and use the duck blood for famous French pressed duck. It becomes a special treat to watch headwaiters in fine restaurants prepare the duck sauce with the press right at the table. A similar press technique may be achieved at home by cutting up the duck carcass and forcing it through a food chopper using the coarse blade. The extracted juices should be strained before using to obtain a better-looking, clearer gravy.

DUCK SAUCE—A Chinese sweet sauce, similar to chutney, made of fruits and served with roast duck and pork, spareribs, and egg roll. More correctly called *duk* sauce, it has a base of apricots, peaches, or plums with spices, sugar, and vinegar added.

The tangy sauce is often served in small dishes, sometimes combined with a mustard, in which the foods may be dipped.

Grandma would be envious of this hearty hot dumpling dish. Carrots, lima beans, and lamb cubes with seasoned tomato sauce and dumplings combine in Lamb Stew 'n Dumplings.

Duck sauce is found in supermarkets or specialty shops in jars and is available in several different kinds. (See also *Sauce.*)

DU JOUR *(duh zhŏŏr', dōō)* — A French term often found on menus in fine restaurants referring to the food specialty of the day, such as the soup or dessert of the day.

DULSE — A coarse, edible seaweed of the red seaweed family found along the continental and island coasts. The salty tang of dulse is acquired from the European and American North Atlantic coasts, as well as the Pacific coast, where it grows abundantly. Children of colonial America considered dulse a candy treat. Alfred W. McCann discovered from observation that healthy old fishermen who were receiving iodine from the fish that ate seaweed were free from arteriosclerosis.

At the Bay of Fundy of the Grand Manan Islands, dulsing becomes an important industry during the summer months. First, the seaweed is torn loose from the sea bottom and gathered. Then, the fresh, brownish seaweed, often transparent in the sun, is spread on huge, flat rocks to dry. After drying, dulse is packed in barrels and sacks ready for shipment. Dulse is also collected and packaged for shipping in the northern countries of Iceland, Scotland, and the Canadian Maritime Provinces.

Because dulse is grown in the sea, it is very rich in iodine. The salty, pleasing taste of dried dulse makes it desirable as a natural candy. It can be cooked like a vegetable and is popular as a relish along the coastal regions. Dulse, also known as carrageen or Irish moss, is used as a thickening agent and can be found in a great many commercial products.

DUMPLING — 1. Light, tender balls of leavened dough steamed or boiled with stews or soups. 2. Pastry-wrapped fruits, often accompanied with a sauce, served as a dessert along with the main course.

The Chinese dumpling, *chu-pao-pa*, developed thousands of years ago, was the beginning of the now universal food. These Chinese dumplings were eaten in soups or with sauces in much the same way as they are eaten today.

The Western world quickly adopted the dumpling as they heard of it from world travelers. It soon became an integral part of English and Scandinavian cookery.

There are as many types of dumplings as there are countries with traditional foods. Dumplings are ravioli in Italy, and, except for the filling, they resemble the *won ton* of China. In Germany, they are either *Kloësse, Knodel,* or *Spaetzle*, depending on the type. Dumplings are *kolodny* in Lithuania, and *Knedliky* in Czechoslovakia, *blintzes* in Slavic countries, and tamales or empanadas in countries where Spanish is spoken. Dumplings are one of the most accepted foods in the world.

In America, stewed dumplings and baked fruit dumplings are favorite menu items for many families. Plump dumplings of flour, cornmeal, cracker meal, or farina are great stew toppers. They are also excellent in soups and ragouts, or served with creamed chicken and pot roasts.

Baked fruit dumplings are a dessert specialty for any time of the year. For the mouth-watering filling, plentiful fresh fruits can be used during the summer months and convenient canned fruits in the cold, winter months.

Dip tablespoon into hot stew liquid before dropping dumplings each time. The dumplings will slide off onto meat and vegetables.

Most dumplings are grouped into one of three categories: boiled, steamed, or baked. Boiled dumplings, drop or molded, are cooked, covered or uncovered, in a simmering liquid. A slightly sweet dumpling batter is used to make drop dumplings. Some drop dumplings are cooked, uncovered, atop the simmering liquid and some in a tightly covered kettle. The liquid in which the dumplings are cooked serves as a sauce for the dumplings when served.

The molded type of boiled dumpling is often rolled and cut out of a potato dumpling dough. However, if you wish, you can shape the dough around a piece of fruit first and then drop it into the boiling water and cook it until it is done.

A steamed dumpling is made from biscuit dough. After the dough has been cut, it is most often shaped around a piece of fruit. The dumplings are then cooked over steam either in custard cups or a perforated pan. Serve steamed dumplings with a rich cream or a sauce.

Baked dumplings, apple dumplings being a good example, are made of plain pastry or a rich biscuit dough. The dough is wrapped around the fruit and placed on a baking sheet to bake. The dumpling can be poached in the oven by setting it in a shallow pan containing a thin syrup.

Beef and Dumplings

      1 beaten egg
      1 10½-ounce can condensed cream
         of celery soup
    ½ cup soft bread crumbs
      2 tablespoons dry onion soup mix
      1 pound ground beef
                • • •
      2 tablespoons shortening
      1 tablespoon all-purpose flour
    ½ teaspoon paprika
    ½ cup water
      1 3-ounce can chopped mushrooms,
         undrained (⅔ cup)
         Dumplings

Combine egg, ¼ *cup* of the soup, crumbs, and dry soup mix. Add beef; mix well. Shape into 8 meatballs. In skillet brown meatballs in hot shortening. Drain off excess fat. Blend together remaining soup, flour, and paprika. Gradually stir in water. Add mushrooms with liquid. Pour over meatballs in *skillet*. Bring to boiling; reduce heat and simmer, covered, for 20 minutes. Pour into 1½-quart casserole. Top with Dumplings. Bake, uncovered, at 400° for 20 to 25 minutes. Makes 4 servings.

Dumplings: Combine 1 cup sifted all-purpose flour, 2 teaspoons baking powder, 1 teaspoon dry onion soup mix, and ¼ teaspoon celery salt. Combine ½ cup milk and 1 tablespoon salad oil. Stir into flour mixture till smooth. Combine 1 cup soft bread crumbs with 2 tablespoons melted butter. Divide dough into 8 portions; drop by tablespoon into buttered crumbs, turning to coat all sides. At serving time place dumplings atop the *boiling* meat mixture.

Lamb Stew 'n Dumplings

      2 pounds boneless lamb shoulder,
         cut in 1-inch cubes
    ¼ cup all-purpose flour
      1 teaspoon paprika
    ¼ teaspoon pepper
      2 tablespoons shortening
      1 8-ounce can tomato sauce
      1 clove garlic, minced
    ½ teaspoon dried thyme leaves,
         crushed
    ½ teaspoon dried marjoram leaves,
         crushed
      1 10-ounce package frozen baby
         lima beans
      6 medium carrots, cut in ½-inch
         pieces
      6 small whole onions
    ⅓ cup milk
      1 cup packaged biscuit mix

Coat lamb cubes with mixture of flour, 2 teaspoons salt, paprika, and pepper. Heat shortening; brown meat. Add 2 cups water, tomato sauce, minced garlic, thyme, and marjoram.

Cover and simmer till meat is almost tender, about 1 hour. Add frozen baby limas, carrots, and onions; cover and simmer until the lamb is very tender, about 20 minutes.

Top with 10 to 12 small Dumplings: Add milk to packaged biscuit mix. Mix well; spoon over hot bubbling stew. Cook, uncovered, over low heat 5 minutes. Cover and cook 10 minutes. Makes 6 to 8 servings.

Chicken with Raisin Dumplings

    1 5- to 6-pound ready-to-cook
       stewing chicken, cut up, *or* 2
       large broiler-fryer chickens,
       cut up
    2 sprigs parsley
    4 stalks celery with leaves
    1 carrot, sliced
    1 small onion, cut up
    2 teaspoons salt
  1/4 teaspoon pepper

    · · ·

    1 cup all-purpose flour
    3 teaspoons baking powder
    1 tablespoon shortening
  1/2 cup raisins
    1 cup coarse dry bread crumbs
    1 beaten egg
  3/4 cup milk
    2 teaspoons grated onion

Place chicken pieces in Dutch oven or large kettle with enough water to cover (about 2 quarts). Add parsley sprigs, celery, sliced carrot, onion, salt, and pepper. Cover mixture; bring to boiling and cook over low heat till tender, about 2 1/2 hours.

Sift together flour, baking powder, and 1 teaspoon salt. Cut shortening into dry ingredients. Add raisins and bread crumbs. Combine egg, milk, and grated onion. Add to raisin mixture; mix just to moisten.

Drop dumpling mixture from tablespoon atop stewed chicken in boiling stock. Cover tightly (don't lift cover); simmer 20 minutes. Remove chicken and dumplings; thicken broth.

Fluffy Dumplings

    1 cup sifted all-purpose flour
    2 teaspoons baking powder
  1/2 teaspoon salt
  1/2 cup milk
    2 tablespoons salad oil

Sift flour, baking powder, and salt together in bowl. Combine milk and oil; add all at once to dry ingredients, stirring till moistened. Drop from tablespoon atop bubbling stew. Cover tightly; let mixture return to boiling. Reduce heat (don't lift cover); simmer 12 to 15 minutes. Makes about 10 dumplings.

Easy Dumplings

  2/3 cup milk
    2 cups packaged biscuit mix

Add milk to package biscuit mix all at once; stir just till mixture is moistened. Drop by rounded tablespoon atop hot, bubbling stew. Cook, uncovered, over low heat 10 minutes. Cover and cook 10 minutes longer, allowing the dumplings to rise, or till done. Makes 10 to 12 meal-perfect Easy Dumplings.

Skillet Strawberry Dumplings

    1 21-ounce can strawberry pie
       filling
 1 1/2 cups orange juice
    1 cup water
  1/4 cup sugar
    1 tablespoon butter or margarine
      Few drops red food coloring
 1 1/2 cups sifted all-purpose flour
  1/3 cup sugar
    1 tablespoon baking powder
  2/3 cup milk
    2 tablespoons salad oil
      Ground cinnamon *or* nutmeg

In electric skillet combine first 5 ingredients. Heat to boiling. Add red food coloring. In mixing bowl sift together flour, the 1/3 cup sugar, baking powder, and 1/2 teaspoon salt. Stir in milk and oil. Drop in 6 portions onto boiling fruit mixture. Sprinkle lightly with cinnamon or nutmeg. Cover; cook at 200° for 10 to 12 minutes or till dumplings are done. Serve warm with cream, if desired. Makes 6 servings.

Fruit with Dumplings

Combine one 8-ounce can fruit cocktail, 1 tablespoon sugar, 1 teaspoon butter or margarine, and 1 teaspoon lemon juice in saucepan. Bring to boil. In small bowl sift together 1/2 cup all-purpose flour, 2 tablespoons sugar, 1 teaspoon baking powder, and 1/4 teaspoon salt. Stir in 1/4 cup milk and 1 teaspoon salad oil.

Drop in 2 portions onto *boiling hot* fruit. Sprinkle lightly with ground cinnamon or ground nutmeg. Cover; cook over medium heat for 10 minutes. Serve with cream. Serves 2.

Stir up dumplings while blueberry sauce is cooking. Dovetailing, or doing two jobs at once, makes the dessert faster and easier.

Drop rounded tablespoons of dumpling batter onto the bubbling blueberry sauce. Dip spoon into hot sauce before each dumpling.

Leave the lid on and avoid peeking while the dumplings cook. Serve light and tender Blueberry Dumplings hot with cream.

Berry-filled fruit dumplings become summer fresh fruit favorites and add a warm glow to winter months using canned or dried fruits. Biscuit dough is most often used to wrap the delectable fruit and spices. Fruit dumplings are usually baked on a baking sheet but can be set in a shallow pan or allowed to poach in their own juices. Rich cream, ice cream, or sweet sauces may accompany the dumplings. (See also *Dessert*.)

Blueberry Dumplings

    1 20-ounce can frozen sweetened
        blueberries (2½ cups)
      Dash salt
    ¼ cup water
    1 tablespoon lemon juice
    1 cup sifted all-purpose flour
    2 tablespoons sugar
    2 teaspoons baking powder
    ¼ teaspoon salt
    1 tablespoon butter
    ½ cup milk

In large saucepan bring frozen, sweetened blueberries, dash salt, and water to boiling. Add lemon juice. Sift together flour, sugar, baking powder, and ¼ teaspoon salt; cut in butter till mixture resembles coarse meal. Add milk all at once, stirring till flour is moistened. Drop batter from tip of tablespoon into bubbling sauce, making 6 dumplings—don't let them overlap. Cover tightly; cook over low heat 10 minutes without uncovering. Serve hot. If desired, serve with cream. Makes 6 servings.

Basic Apple Dumplings

As good as the ones grandma used to make—

1½ cups sugar
1½ cups water
¼ teaspoon ground cinnamon
¼ teaspoon ground nutmeg
8 drops red food coloring
3 tablespoons butter or margarine
. . .
2 cups sifted all-purpose flour
2 teaspoons baking powder
1 teaspoon salt
⅔ cup shortening
½ cup milk
6 medium, whole apples, peeled and cored

For syrup mix sugar, water, cinnamon, nutmeg, and red food coloring; bring to boiling. Remove from heat; add butter or margarine.

Sift together flour, baking powder, and salt; cut in shortening till mixture resembles coarse crumbs. Add milk all at once; stir just till flour is moistened. On lightly floured surface, roll to 18x12-inch rectangle.

Cut in six 6-inch squares. Place apple on each*. Sprinkle apples generously with additional sugar, cinnamon, and nutmeg; dot with butter. Moisten edges of pastry. Bring corners to center and pinch edges together.

Place 1 inch apart in *ungreased* 11x7x1½-inch baking pan. Pour syrup over dumplings; sprinkle with sugar. Bake at 375° till apples are tender, about 35 minutes. Serve warm with maple syrup, if desired. Makes 6 servings.

*Or use ½ apple, sliced, in each square.

Spice-Prune Dumplings

½ pound dried prunes
   (about 1½ cups)
½ cup sugar
¼ cup chopped walnuts
2 tablespoons butter or margarine
1 tablespoon lemon juice
¼ teaspoon ground cinnamon
½ teaspoon ground nutmeg
2 cups biscuit mix
½ cup water
½ teaspoon ground cinnamon
¼ teaspoon ground nutmeg

In saucepan combine prunes with 3 cups water. Cover; bring to boiling and boil gently 20 minutes. Add sugar and cook, covered, 5 minutes more. Drain and reserve liquid (about 2 cups). Pit and chop prunes. Combine prunes with ½ cup water and cook till excess liquid is absorbed, about 2 minutes. Stir in walnuts, butter or margarine, lemon juice, ¼ teaspoon ground cinnamon, and ¼ teaspoon ground nutmeg.

Combine biscuit mix and ½ cup water; stir till dry ingredients are moistened. Turn onto floured surface and knead lightly 8 to 10 times. Roll into a 16x8-inch rectangle; cut into eight 4-inch squares. Place 2 tablespoons prune mixture in center of each square. Fold corners of dough to center and pinch edges together. Place in 12x7½x2-inch baking dish. Stir the remaining cinnamon and nutmeg into reserved prune liquid; pour over dumplings. Sprinkle dumplings with additional granulated sugar. Bake at 375° for 30 to 35 minutes. Serve warm with cream, if desired. Makes 8 servings.

Peach-Cheese Dumplings

1 29-ounce can peach halves
1½ cups sifted all-purpose flour
¾ teaspoon salt
½ cup shortening
½ cup shredded sharp process American cheese
Butter
Ground cinnamon
Lemon Sauce

Drain peaches, reserving 1 cup syrup. Sift flour with salt; cut in shortening till size of small peas. Add cheese; mix lightly. Blend in 3 to 4 tablespoons cold water as for pastry.

Roll dough on lightly floured surface to 18x12-inch rectangle. Cut in six 6-inch squares. Place peach half, cut side down, in center of each square. Dot with butter; dash with cinnamon. Moisten edges of pastry and fold over peach, pinching to seal. Place dumplings on *ungreased* baking sheet. Bake at 425° for 20 to 25 minutes. Makes 6 servings.

Serve with *Lemon Sauce:* In saucepan blend ¼ cup sugar, 1 tablespoon cornstarch, and dash salt; gradually add 1 cup reserved peach syrup. Cook and stir till thickened and clear. Add 1 teaspoon grated lemon peel, 1 tablespoon lemon juice, 1 tablespoon butter.

DUNGENESS CRAB *(duhn' juh nes)* — A large, reddish crab. These crabs, named for a town in Washington, live along the Pacific coast shores from Mexico to Alaska. They weigh from 1½ to 3½ pounds and are prized for their rich, tender meat.

Dungeness crabs are available on the markets in many forms—live, cooked in the shell, fresh cooked meat, frozen meat, and canned meat. The meat comes from both the body and the claws.

State laws prevent these crabs being sold in the soft-shell stage. (See also *Crab*.)

DUNLOP CHEESE — A sweet, rich, firm, white cheese that resembles Cheddar cheese. At one time Dunlop was regarded as Scotland's national cheese.

DURUM WHEAT *(door' uhm)* — A type of wheat also known as macaroni wheat. Durum is classified as a very hard wheat and is used in making pasta, such as macaroni, spaghetti, and noodles.

Durum wheat originally grew in Southwestern Asia and in the Balkan areas around the Mediterranean Sea. From there it was introduced into those sections of the world that had little rainfall. In the United States, Minnesota, Montana, and the Dakotas have become the principal areas where this wheat is raised.

For centuries, man has used this amber-colored grain to make pasta products. The characteristics that have made durum wheat desirable for pasta are its ability to become tender when cooked, yet hold its shape without a gummy or sticky texture; a nutty flavor; and a pleasing yellow color in the cooked food.

Durum wheat kernels are transformed into pasta by separating the bran and germ sections of the kernel. Then the remainder is ground into a coarse meal, called semolina. Water is mixed with semolina to make a dough. Sometimes, salt, flavoring, B vitamins, and iron are added for flavor and enrichment. This stiff mixture is then formed into one of the more than 150 different pasta shapes made for today's market. (See also *Wheat*.)

DUST — To sprinkle a dry ingredient *lightly* over food. Typical dusting ingredients are granulated sugar, confectioners' sugar, flour, and various spices. They are dusted over desserts, meats, and breads as a coating or as a garnish. The dry ingredients can be sprinkled from a spoon or sifted through a sifter or through a sieve. This latter method gives a finer, more even coating over the food.

Interesting decorations can be made by dusting sugar or spice in a design. Place a doily or stencil over the food and then dust. Carefully pick up the stencil so the design will not be disturbed.

When a heavy coating of flour or sugar is spread over the food, this is known as dredging rather than dusting.

DUTCH OVEN — A deep, heavy pan with a tight-fitting lid. Dutch ovens come in a wide range of sizes and are made of metals, such as aluminum, cast iron, and stainless steel. They may be used either in the oven or on top of the range. Electric models are also available for cooking in the kitchen, dining room, or patio.

The Dutch oven's large size and tight-fitting lid make it suitable for braising pot roasts, cooking stews, steaming foods, deep-fat frying, warming buns and rolls, and popping corn. It can also double as a saucepan when the supply of equipment is limited or an extra large saucepan is needed for preparing a large recipe. (See also *Pots and Pans*.)

DUTCH-PROCESS COCOA — A rich, dark cocoa powder treated with alkaline salt. The Dutch people in the East Indies discovered that cocoa was improved when treated with the salt. This cocoa has a darker color and less acid flavor than does regular cocoa, and has a delicate aroma. It blends well with liquids and does not separate easily. (See also *Cocoa*.)

DUXELLES *(dûk sel', duhk-, dook)* — A mixture of mushrooms, shallots, and herbs. The mushrooms and shallots are minced and cooked with the herbs in a stock until reduced to a paste or dried out.

Duxelles, usually associated with French cookery, can be used as a garnish or as a flavoring ingredient with sauces, stuffings, or meats. (See also *French Cookery*.)

E

EASTER — The annual celebration of the resurrection of Jesus Christ in the Christian religion. Easter comes in the spring of the year near the time of ancient pagan spring festivals and the Jewish Passover. Therefore, many of the traditional practices, symbols, and foods are related to those of other religions and cultures.

The English word, Easter, is derived from the name of the Anglo-Saxon goddess of spring, Eostre or Ostâra. The word for Easter in many other languages comes from the Hebrew word for Passover.

The exact date of Easter is variable, coming on a Sunday between March 22 and April 25. For those who want to figure the date for themselves, Easter comes on the first Sunday after the first full moon following March 21. These complicated calculations were arrived at centuries ago after much controversy over what calendar to use, whether the date would vary, and if Easter would always be on Sunday.

Easter has a number of traditional foods as do all holidays. Some of these foods reflect a significance of the holiday and others are inherited from ancient cultures. Breads and cakes of all sorts, meats, such as lamb and ham, and eggs are among the most vivid examples of Easter foods.

Breads: Yeast breads, rolls, buns, and coffee cakes are a significant part of the Easter celebration. Many times they are formed into symbolic shapes of rabbits, lambs, and crosses. In some countries, days of baking precede Easter Sunday and then the goods are taken to the church to be blessed before they are eaten.

Each country has its own bread that is traditionally made for Easter. The Russians bake a high, round yeast bread called *kulich.* This is served with *paskha,* a sweet cottage cheese dessert shaped like a pyramid. The Greeks make *tsoureki,* which is a braided yeast bread with brightly colored eggs arranged in the center. Other breads, familiar to Americans, are the *stollen* made in Germany and Austria, the golden bread in Ireland, the *babka* in Poland, and the *mazanetz* of Czechoslovakia.

In America one of the better-known breads is the hot cross bun. This round bun has raisins in the dough and a cross on the top made of white frosting. These are eaten during Lent, on Good Friday, and on Easter. They are traditionally broken open rather than cut open.

Breads from all over the world have been adapted to America's typical Easter menus. Large dinners at noon or in the evening usually include hot bread, buns, or rolls. Brunches, which are especially good to have after early church services, feature coffee cakes or coffee breads, sweet rolls, or buns among the holiday foods.

❧ •MENU• ❧

EASTER MORNING BRUNCH
Chilled Tomato Juice
Canadian Bacon   Sausage Links
Scrambled Eggs
Easter Nest Coffee Cake or
Spring Flower Rolls
Coffee   Tea

Spring Flower Rolls

      1 package active dry yeast
   2¾ to 3¼ cups sifted all-purpose
         flour
         . . .
      ¾ cup milk
      ¼ cup butter or margarine
      2 tablespoons sugar
      ½ teaspoon salt
      1 slightly beaten egg
         Jams and preserves
         Butter or margarine, melted

In large mixer bowl combine yeast and *1¼ cups* flour. Heat milk, butter, sugar, and salt just till warm, stirring occasionally to melt butter. Add to dry mixture in mixing bowl; add egg. Beat at low speed with electric mixer for ½ minute, scraping sides of bowl constantly. Beat 3 minutes at high speed. By hand, stir in enough of the remaining flour to make a soft dough. Turn out on flour surface; knead till smooth and elastic, about 8 to 10 minutes. Place in lightly greased bowl, turning once to grease surface. Cover; let rise in warm place till double, about 1 hour.

Punch down. Cover; let rest 10 minutes. On lightly floured surface, roll dough to ¼-inch thickness; cut with floured 1¼-inch biscuit cutter. Grease muffin cups (about 2½ inches across); arrange 5 circles of dough, petal fashion, around sides of cup; place 1 in center.

Cover; let almost double (about 30 minutes). Lightly poke down center of each roll and fill with colorful jams and preserves.

Bake at 400° for 10 to 15 minutes. Brush with melted butter. Makes about 16 rolls.

Easter Nest Coffee Cake

      1 package active dry yeast
      3 cups sifted all-purpose flour
      ¾ cup milk
      ¼ cup sugar
      ¼ cup shortening
      1 teaspoon salt
      1 slightly beaten egg
         Shredded coconut
         Green food coloring
         Confectioners' Sugar Icing
         Candy decorations

In large mixer bowl combine yeast and *1½ cups* flour. Heat milk, sugar, shortening, and salt just till warm, stirring to melt shortening. Add to dry mixture; add egg. Beat at low speed with an electric mixer for ½ minute, scraping sides of bowl constantly. Beat 3 minutes at high speed. By hand, stir in enough of the remaining flour to make a soft dough. On floured surface, knead till smooth and elastic, 8 to 10 minutes. Place in greased bowl, turning to grease surface. Cover; let rise in warm place till double, about 1 hour. Punch down; divide in thirds. Cover; let rest 10 minutes.

Shape one-third of dough in 6 "eggs"; place close together in center of greased baking sheet. For "nest", shape remaining dough in two 26-inch ropes; twist together. Coil around "eggs"; seal ends. Cover; let rise till double (about 1 hour). Bake at 375° for 15 to 20 minutes. Cool.

Tint coconut with a few drops of food coloring. Frost coffee cake with Confectioners' Sugar Icing made by blending light cream with confectioners' sugar till of spreading consistency; sprinkle "eggs" with candy decorations, the "nest" with tinted coconut.

Meats: Various meats including turkey, both fresh and smoked pork, and lamb are traditional Easter fare. Pork has been served for centuries as a symbol of luck and lamb has religious symbolism.

Going on an Easter egg hunt

Discovering this nest of eggs delights both →
children and adults. Easter Nest Coffee Cake, made of sweet dough, is gaily frosted.

❈MENU❈

EASTER DINNER
Appetizer Relish Tray
Baked Ham with Apricots
Green Beans Amandine   *Gelatin Salad*
Bunny Rolls   *Butter*
Orange Cream Cake
Coffee   *Tea*

Bunny Rolls

 1 package active dry yeast
 5 to 5½ cups sifted all-purpose
   flour
1¼ cups milk
 ½ cup shortening
 ⅓ cup sugar
 1 teaspoon salt
 2 beaten eggs
 2 tablespoons grated orange peel
 ¼ cup orange juice
         .   .   .
 2 cups sifted confectioners' sugar
 ¼ cup hot water
 1 teaspoon butter or margarine

In large mixer bowl combine yeast and *2¾ cups* flour. Heat milk, shortening, sugar, and salt just till warm, stirring occasionally to melt shortening. Add to dry mixture in mixing bowl; add eggs, orange peel, and orange juice. Beat at low speed with electric mixer for ½ minute, scraping sides of bowl constantly. Beat 3 minutes at high speed. By hand, stir in enough of the remaining flour to make a soft dough. Turn out on a lightly floured surface and knead till smooth and elastic, 8 or 10 minutes. Place dough in a greased bowl, turning once to grease surface. Cover and let rise in warm place till double, about 2 hours. Punch down; cover and let rest 10 minutes.

To shape: on lightly floured surface, roll dough in rectangle ½ inch thick. Cut dough in strips ½ inch wide and roll between hands to smooth into rope like strips.

For curlicue bunnies: For each bunny, use a 10-inch strip of dough for the body and a 5-inch strip for the head. On a lightly greased baking sheet, make a loose pinwheel of strip for body. Make smaller pinwheel for head and place close to body. (They'll "grow" together as dough rises.) For ears, pinch off 1½-inch strips and roll between hands till smooth and pointed at both ends. For ears: snip off both points and place next to head. Pinch off a bit of dough and roll in ball for tail.

For twist bunnies: For each bunny, use a 14-inch strip of dough. On a lightly greased baking sheet, make a figure 8 of one strip of dough. Instead of sealing ends, overlap, then spread apart to make ears. Roll small ball of dough for tail; place atop dough at bottom of figure 8.

Cover bunnies; let rise till nearly double in size, about 45 to 60 minutes. Bake at 375° for an additional 12 to 15 minutes.

For confectioners' sugar glaze: combine confectioners' sugar, hot water, and butter; beat till smooth and well blended. Brush over bunnies while warm. Makes about 30 rolls.

Orange Cream Cake

2½ cups sifted cake flour
1⅔ cups sugar
3½ teaspoons baking powder
 1 teaspoon salt
 2 teaspoons grated orange peel
 ¾ cup orange juice
 ⅔ cup shortening
 3 eggs
 ⅓ cup water
 ¼ teaspoon almond extract
   Orange Cream Frosting
   Small candy Easter eggs

Into large mixer bowl sift together dry ingredients; add peel, juice, and shortening. Beat 2 minutes at medium speed with electric mixer. Add eggs, ⅓ cup water, and extract; beat 2 minutes more. Pour into greased and floured 13x9x2-inch baking pan. Bake at 350° for 40 to 45 minutes. Cool in pan. Top with frosting. Cut in squares; top with candy Easter eggs.

Orange Cream Frosting: Combine 3 cups sifted confectioners' sugar, ⅓ cup shortening, ½ teaspoon shredded orange peel, ¼ cup *hot* orange juice, 1 teaspoon lemon juice, and dash salt. If desired, add a few drops yellow food coloring. Beat with mixer at high speed till smooth. Add more confectioners' sugar, if needed.

Eggs: Eggs have long been a symbol of new life. Anyone that has seen an egg crack open and a baby chick appear can understand why this was chosen by many early cultures and carried over into our Easter tradition to depict new life.

The custom of giving eggs, dying them, and playing games with eggs are a part of Easter heritage. The early Egyptians, Persians, Greeks, Romans, and Gauls gave eggs as gifts during their spring festivals. This is still a practice with many families around the world today.

Eggs were originally painted to represent the rays of the sun or the colors of spring. Today, children delight in helping to dye eggs for Easter baskets and egg hunts. These gay eggs also make attractive centerpieces and garnishes for meat platters.

There are commercial dyes on sale to use with hard-cooked or blown eggs. For an even color, rinse the eggs in hot water and dry just before dipping in the dye. Peeled eggs can also be dyed. Use food coloring and fruit-flavored drink powder for eggs which will be colorful and edible.

Colored Easter Eggs

Garnish meat platter with colorful, peeled eggs—

Hard-cook eggs by placing eggs in saucepan and covering with cold water (at least 1 inch above egg). Rapidly bring to boiling; reduce heat to keep water just *below simmering.* Cover; cook 15 to 20 minutes. Cool at once in cold water—this helps prevent dark surface on yolk and makes peeling easier. To shell, crack shell all over, then roll between hands to loosen. Start peeling at large end where air pocket is.

To color eggs: For a variety of colors, in separate bowls dissolve 1 envelope of each of the following fruit-flavored drink powders: orange, cherry, strawberry, grape, and lemon-lime in ½ cup water. Add eggs and tint to desired color. By leaving some eggs in longer than others, you'll obtain different shades of the same hue. Drain eggs on paper toweling.

For bright yellow eggs add ¼ teaspoon yellow food coloring to ½ cup water; tint eggs, then dip briefly in solution of 1 envelope orange-drink powder in ½ cup water. For blue or green eggs use blue or green food coloring in water.

Tint peeled eggs and pipe on cream cheese. Use Colored Easter Eggs for a garnish.

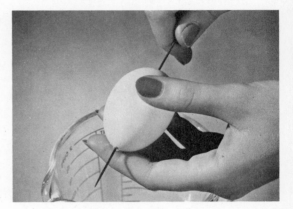

To blow shell: wash egg, puncture each end with pin, enlarge hole slightly, run pin through egg to break yolk. Over a cup, blow gently in one hole. Rinse, dry, and dye shell.

Hard cook eggs; dry. Dip warm eggs into dye prepared according to package directions. Dry on rack; polish with wax or oil.

Eggs are also the focal point of Easter games. Brightly colored, hard-cooked eggs are hidden and children search for them in annual egg hunts. Rolling eggs is an English custom which Americans have adopted. President Madison initiated the egg roll on the White House lawn during his term from 1808 to 1812. This event has become an annual affair at the capitol.

The colored eggs should be returned to the refrigerator as soon as the games are finished. Used in various ways, these are good as creamed eggs or goldenrod eggs for breakfast, as a main dish for lunch, deviled, pickled, in potato salad, and in Thousand Island dressing.

❈MENU❈

AFTER THE HUNT LUNCH
Ham 'n Egg Triple Deckers
Pineapple-Cheese Salad   Corn Chips
Honey-Pecan Cake
Milk

Ham 'n Egg Triple Deckers

  2 hard-cooked eggs, shelled
1½ cups ground cooked ham
  2 tablespoons chopped green
     pepper
  1 tablespoon prepared mustard
  3 tablespoons mayonnaise
12 slices white bread
   Butter or margarine

Chop eggs. Combine eggs, ham, green pepper, and mustard. Mix well. Stir in mayonnaise. Spread one side of each slice bread with butter or margarine. Divide *half* of the ham mixture among four slices of bread; spread evenly. Cover each with another slice bread; spread each with remaining ham mixture. Top with remaining bread slices, buttered side down.

Brush the outside of sandwiches with melted butter. Place on baking sheet; bake at 375° till brown, 15 to 20 minutes. Serves 4.

Pineapple-Cheese Salad

  1 20½-ounce can pineapple chunks
  1 16-ounce carton cream-style
     cottage cheese (2 cups)
  2 cups miniature marshmallows
½ cup pitted dates, snipped
  1 tablespoon lemon juice
   Lettuce

Drain pineapple, reserving ¼ cup syrup. Combine reserved syrup and next 4 ingredients. Mound cheese mixture on lettuce-lined plates; arrange pineapple chunks around. Top each with one whole pitted date. Serves 6 to 8.

Honey-Pecan Cake

  1 tablespoon vinegar
   Milk
  1 cup salad oil
1½ cups sugar
  3 eggs
  1 teaspoon vanilla
  2 cups sifted all-purpose flour
  3 teaspoons baking powder
½ teaspoon baking soda
  1 teaspoon ground cinnamon
¼ teaspoon ground cloves
½ cup chopped pecans
   Honey Syrup

Combine vinegar and enough milk to make 1 cup; set aside. Stir salad oil into sugar; add eggs and vanilla. Beat 1 minute at medium speed with electric mixer. Sift flour, baking powder, baking soda, cinnamon, and cloves together. Add to creamed mixture alternately with milk mixture. Beat the mixture for 1 minute more. Stir in all the pecans.

Pour into greased and floured 10-inch fluted tube pan. Bake at 350° for 40 minutes. Let stand 10 minutes. Remove from pan. Prick holes in hot cake; drizzle with Honey Syrup.

Honey Syrup: Boil ¼ cup honey, 1 tablespoon water, and 1 tablespoon lemon juice.

EAU DE VIE (*ō′ duh vē′*) —The French term for brandy. Sometimes the term is extended to identify the fruit used in distilling the brandy. For example, *eau de vie de cidre* is apple brandy. (See also *Brandy*.)

ÉCLAIR *(ā klâr′, i klâr′, ā′ klâr)* — An oblong pastry shell with a sweet filling inside and a frosting or glaze over the outside. Éclairs are made from a dough much like cream puff dough. However, éclairs are piped through a pastry tube into finger shape, as well as being dropped from a spoon like the cream puff. Éclairs are served as a refreshment or dessert.

The typical éclair has a creamy filling of whipped cream, ice cream, or custard and a chocolate, vanilla, or coffee icing.

Éclairs

    ½ cup butter or margarine
    1 cup sifted all-purpose flour
    ¼ teaspoon salt
    4 eggs
      Chocolate Icing (optional)
      French Custard Filling

Melt butter in 1 cup boiling water. Add flour and salt all at once; stir vigorously. Cook and stir till mixture forms a ball that doesn't separate. Remove from heat; cool slightly. Add eggs one at a time; beat well after each.

Put dough through a pastry tube or paper cone making 4-inch strips, ¾ inch wide on a greased baking sheet. Bake at 450° for 15 minutes, then at 325° for 25 minutes. Remove from oven; split. Turn oven off; put éclairs back in to dry, about 20 minutes. Cool on rack. Frost tops, if desired. Just before serving, fill each with custard. Makes 14.

French Custard Filling: In saucepan, combine ⅔ cup sugar, 2 tablespoons all-purpose flour, 2 tablespoons cornstarch, and ½ teaspoon salt. Gradually stir in 3 cups milk. Cook and stir till mixture thickens and boils; cook and stir 2 to 3 minutes longer. Stir a little hot mixture into 2 slightly beaten egg yolks; return to hot mixture. Cook and stir just till mixture boils. Add 2 teaspoons vanilla; cool. Beat smooth. Whip 1 cup cream; fold into custard.

The grand finale

Make éclairs ahead, fill with vanilla or coffee ice cream, and freeze. At serving time, top with bold-flavored pecan sauce.

You can vary the basic éclair by flavoring with coffee, chocolate, or fruit; making the filling with a mix; or topping the éclair with a sauce. (See *Cream Puff, Dessert* for additional information.)

Coffee-Ice Cream Éclairs

Taste as good as they look—

½ cup butter or margarine
1 cup boiling water
1 cup sifted all-purpose flour
4 eggs
1 quart vanilla or coffee ice cream

. . .

1 cup light corn syrup
1 tablespoon instant coffee powder
3 tablespoons cornstarch
2 tablespoons butter or margarine
1 teaspoon vanilla
½ cup chopped pecans

In saucepan combine the ½ cup butter and boiling water; bring to boiling. Add flour all at once, stirring rapidly. Reduce heat. Cook and stir till mixture leaves sides of pan and gathers around spoon in smooth, compact mass. Remove from heat. Add eggs, one at a time; beat vigorously after each addition. Continue beating till mixture looks satiny and breaks off when spoon is raised.

Using about ¼ cup dough for each éclair, drop from spoon onto *ungreased* baking sheet about 2 inches apart, leaving about 6 inches between rows. With small spatula, shape each mound into a 4x1-inch rectangle, rounding sides and piling dough on top.

Bake at 400° till golden brown and puffy, about 40 minutes. Cool on rack. Cut each éclair in half lengthwise and remove webbing.

Fill bottom halves with ice cream; replace tops. Keep in freezer till serving time. Serve with sauce. Makes 10 to 12.

Coffee-Pecan Sauce: Measure corn syrup into medium saucepan. Combine 1½ cups water and coffee powder; blend in cornstarch. Stir into corn syrup in pan. Cook and stir till sauce thickens and boils. Remove from heat; add the 2 tablespoons butter and vanilla. Stir till butter melts; add pecans. Makes 2½ cups sauce.

Hurry-Up Éclairs

½ cup butter or margarine
1 cup sifted all-purpose flour
¼ teaspoon salt
4 eggs
1 3- or 3¼-ounce package *regular* vanilla pudding mix
1 cup whipping cream
½ teaspoon vanilla
Sifted confectioners' sugar
1 slightly beaten egg white
Small multi-colored decorative candies

Melt butter in 1 cup boiling water. Add flour and salt all at once; stir vigorously. Cook and stir till mixture forms a ball that doesn't separate. Remove from heat; cool slightly. Add eggs, one at a time, beating well after each till smooth. Put through a pastry tube or paper cone making 4-inch strips, ¾ inch wide on greased cookie sheet.

Bake at 450° for 15 minutes, then at 325° for 25 minutes. Remove from oven; split. Turn oven off; put éclairs back in to dry about 20 minutes. Cool on rack.

Using only 1¾ cups milk, prepare pudding mix according to package directions; chill. Whip cream. Beat pudding smooth; fold in whipping cream and vanilla. Fill éclairs.

Add enough sifted confectioners' sugar to the egg white to make frosting of spreading consistency (about 1¼ cups). Frost tops of éclairs and sprinkle with decorative candies for confetti effect. Chill till serving time. Makes about 14 éclairs.

ÉCREVISSE (*ā kruh vēs'*) — The French name for crayfish. (See also *Crayfish*.)

Slice red "cannon balls" of Edam to find milk cheese.

EDAM CHEESE *(ē' duhm, ē' dam)* — A mild, firm cheese usually in a round shape with a bright red covering. It has a smooth texture with no holes and a light, buttery flavor. Edam and Gouda are similar in shape and flavor. However, Edam is made partly with skim milk, while Gouda is made entirely with whole milk.

Edam was named for the town in northern Holland where it was originally made during the Middle Ages. The farmers in Edam began exporting it as early as the thirteenth century and today, it is known and exported throughout the world.

Edam has a shape and color that is the same worldwide. The characteristic red coloring was first used in the thirteenth century. At that time, the farmers agreed to distinguish their cheese by giving a reddish color to the rind. The cheese sold on modern markets still has this covering.

The form is that of a cannonball. This comparison comes from its shape and from legend. Edams, being hard, were supposedly used during a naval battle when the supply of cannonballs was exhausted.

Edam, like other cheeses, is known as a rich source of protein. It also supplies calcium and the B vitamins. A one-ounce serving contains 85 calories.

Use Edam as an appetizer or a dessert, rather than for cooking or grating. Make dips and spreads from the cheese and serve it out of the shell. Just remove the top (cut a design, if desired) and scoop out the cheese. Prepare the mixture and spoon it back into the shell. Desserts of slices of cheese with fruit, for instance oranges and grapes, are quite easy but very elegant to serve. (See also *Cheese.*)

Stuffed Edam

Bring 1 round Edam cheese to room temperature. Cut a 5- or 6-inch star pattern from heavy paper; pin to top of cheese, anchoring points. Cut around star with sharp knife. Remove star; carefully remove cheese from shell. Whip cheese with electric beater adding enough cream to make spreading consistency. Mound mixture in shell. Chill till serving time. Remove from refrigerator about 1 hour before serving. Serve with assorted crackers and apple wedges.

EDGEBONE — The aitchbone or rump bone of an animal. (See also *Meat.*)

EEL — A smooth, slender, elongated fish. Europeans and Americans consider the rich meat of eels to be quite a delicacy.

Eels, like other fish, have fins and scales. The dorsal and anal fins are long; however, there are no pelvic fins. Their minute scales are embedded in the skin. Eels are typically a green to brown color on the back and yellow on the sides.

The mysterious habits of eels have fascinated men for years. At spawning time mature eels from both America and Europe migrate to the sea around Bermuda. When spawning is completed, the eels die. In spring, the young eels, called elvers, migrate to the fresh waters where their parents lived. They live their lives in these waters, eating animal matter and hiding in mud or under rocks, until caught by fisherman or the time arrives to return to the spawning ground.

After being caught, eels are shipped to market in tank trucks which keep them alive. They are sold fresh or processed for sale by canning, pickling, or smoking.

Fresh eel is very perishable, so refrigerate and use it as soon as possible. Before cooking, remove the skin and entrails, wash, and cut into pieces. Poach, broil, marinate, fry, or bake the pieces.

Smoked eel will keep several weeks in the refrigerator. These do not have to be skinned, although skinning does make the food more attractive. Canned and pickled eel can be kept on the kitchen shelf. The supply should be rotated regularly.

Eel is served either hot or cold. Use it as an appetizer, a light lunch, snack, salad ingredient, or part of an entrée with other fish and meat. Tartar sauce, lemon juice and pepper, or mayonnaise served with eel complement the flavor.

Before cooking, eel averages 230 calories per serving and has the B vitamins and vitamin A. Smoked eel has 165 calories, but the vitamins have been lost in processing. (See also *Fish.*)

EELPOUT — Another name for the burbot, a freshwater fish related to the cod; and a small fish found in the Pacific.

EGG

From a poached breakfast egg to a late-night eggnog snack, eggs add flavor to any meal.

Even though the age-old question, "Which came first, the chicken or the egg?" is still being debated, it is a fact that the two are an inseparable pair. By definition, an egg is the hard-shelled reproductive body of an animal. Although other animal eggs are occasionally eaten, the chicken egg is the kind most commonly used in cooking.

The chicken has existed since prehistoric times and today is probably the most widely distributed food animal in the world. For centuries, the chicken egg has been an important food throughout the world. In ancient times, the scarcity of eggs made them a delicacy. For this reason, the Chinese developed a method of preserving eggs for many years in caustic lime—a procedure that still survives today. The egg does not spoil, but the inside shrinks to a dark jellylike substance.

The egg also played a part in superstitions and religions of ancient civilizations. Livia, the wife of the Roman Emperor Augustus, was advised that if she carried an egg under her breast, the sex of the chick that hatched would indicate the sex of her unborn child. Livia followed this advice. Shortly after a young cock was hatched, she gave birth to a son. This coincidence soon led other mothers-to-be to follow this uncomfortable custom.

In religion, many ancient people regarded the egg as a sacred symbol of the world and its elements. To them, each part of the egg represented a specific thing: shell (earth), white (water), yolk (fire), and air cell (air). An early Christian custom considered eggs, blessed by a local priest, to be a holy gift. Even today, gaily painted and decorated eggs are used at Easter as a symbol of the Resurrection.

Parts of the egg: The egg has three main parts—shell, white (albumen), and yolk. Each of these parts can be readily distinguished by the homemaker.

The calcium carbonate shell is a hard semipermeable membrane that makes up about 11 percent of the egg. Although in some areas one color of shell is preferred over another, the shell color is related to the hen's breed and has no effect on the egg's nutritive value or flavor.

The egg white, comprising about 58 percent of the egg, can be divided into thick and thin white. A freshly laid egg has a large amount of thick white. After the egg is laid, chemical action gradually converts the thick white to thin white.

The yolk, which comprises about a third of the egg, is the part that contains the reproductive cell. A very thin membrane separates the yolk from the white. The yolk is anchored in place by cordlike structures called the chalazae. The color of the yolk, ranging from light yellow to greenish yellow, depends on the hen's feed. A double-yolked egg occurs when two yolks drop into the hen's oviduct at the same time or very close together.

Nutritional value: Since the egg must meet the nutritional needs of the chick embryo, it is a compact package of proteins, vitamins, and minerals that can contribute much to the diet. Although the egg's size will affect its caloric value slightly, an average egg has about 75 calories.

A perfect breakfast entrée

← For eggs at their best, serve Soft-Cooked Eggs. After snipping off the top with egg scissors, spoon out the warm, yellow center.

Calcium is the most abundant nutrient in the unshelled egg, but since almost all of this mineral is found in the shell, it provides little nutritionally. In addition to protein and calcium, the egg contains some sodium, phosphorus, iron, thiamine, riboflavin, vitamin A, and vitamin D.

An egg is one of the few natural foods that contain vitamin D. Although fish liver oil is the highest natural source of this vitamin, egg yolk ranks second. In the ordinary diet, eggs, milk, and butter are the major food sources of vitamin D.

Enough eggs are eaten that they make an important nutritional contribution to the American diet. One egg is recommended as an occasional protein substitute for one ounce of cooked lean meat.

How to select: Eggs can be selected according to a grading system established by the U. S. Department of Agriculture. This system applies only to eggs sold in interstate commerce, but most states also maintain these standards for intrastate sales.

The criteria used for grading eggs are: shell condition, white condition, size of air cell, yolk condition, and presence of abnormalities such as blood spots. The grade decreases as the air cell size increases, the white thins, and the yolk flattens and breaks easily after the shell is broken. Depending on their condition, eggs are classified as Grade AA (Fresh Fancy), Grade A, and Grade B.

Since fresh eggs are sold in the shell, they must be graded without breaking this shell. This is done by a process known as candling. Candling consists of using a strong light to view the air cell; the size, position, and mobility of the yolk; and the firmness and clearness of the white. Although a candle was the original source of light for this procedure, today electronic candlers are used.

To ensure quality, the break-out test is often used in combination with candling. Sample eggs from each shipment are broken out on a flat surface where quality is judged by observing the yolk and the height of the thick white. It is assumed that if the broken-out eggs are of the desired quality, then the candling operation must be grading accurately.

Although the grade of an egg is a guide to its appearance and quality, lesser grade eggs are not of a lower nutritive value. As an example, the presence of a blood spot in the egg is sufficient to lower its grade but this in no way detracts from the nutritive quality of the egg. Only the egg's appearance is affected.

Eggs are also grouped according to size. The size categories, based on minimum weight per dozen, are jumbo-30 ounces/dozen, extra large-27 ounces/dozen, large-24 ounces/dozen, medium-21 ounces/dozen, small-18 ounces/dozen, and peewee-15 ounces/dozen. Since the size and grade of an egg are not related, an egg of any size may be of any grade. Recipes usually assume the use of large or medium eggs.

All eggs on the market must have a clean shell, so, if necessary, they are washed before marketing. Since this removes the natural "bloom" or protein coating that seals the pores, the pores are resealed by spraying with a fine mist of colorless, odorless, tasteless mineral oil.

When selecting eggs, look for the label stamped on the egg carton or on the tape sealing of the carton. This gives the size and grade of the eggs and also assures you that the eggs meet USDA standards. When egg appearance or egg white volume is important, use Grade AA or Grade A eggs. These eggs contain a high proportion of thick white and, therefore, when broken do not spread out as much as eggs of a lower grade. Lower grade eggs, however, usually sell at a lower price, and as a result, are a better buy for dishes in which eggs are only one of several ingredients.

Other than shell eggs, both dried and frozen eggs are produced, primarily for use in commercial food services. Dried egg solids have at least 90 percent of the water content removed. They are available as whole egg solids, egg yolk solids, and egg white solids. These are used extensively by the manufacturers of packaged mixes, such as cake mixes.

Frozen eggs are liquid yolks, whites, or whole eggs that are thoroughly combined, then frozen. Frozen eggs should have the USDA inspection seal to assure the consumer that they are prepared from wholesome eggs under sanitary conditions.

Using frozen eggs

Thaw frozen eggs completely in the unopened carton and use them promptly. When using frozen whole eggs or egg yolks, allow for added sugar, corn syrup, or salt. Because of the possible presence of food poisoning organisms, use frozen eggs only in dishes that are cooked thoroughly.

For 1 fresh whole egg
   Substitute 3 tablespoons frozen whole egg, thawed

For 1 fresh egg yolk
   Substitute 4 teaspoons frozen egg yolk, thawed

For 1 fresh egg white
   Substitute 2 tablespoons frozen egg white, thawed

How to store: At home, store eggs in the refrigerator in a covered container, preferably the egg carton. This decreases the absorption of odors as well as keeps the blunt end up, thus reducing the movement of the yolk. Do not wash eggs before storing as this removes the protective coating.

For best flavor and cooking quality, use eggs within one week of purchase. Although there will be some quality deterioration, eggs that have been refrigerated for several weeks are still acceptable when combined with other ingredients.

When a recipe calls for only one part of the egg, yolk or white, tightly cover and refrigerate the leftover portion. Seal egg yolks first by covering them with a layer of cold water. Egg yolks can be stored in this manner for one or two days (drain before using); leftover egg whites will keep for a maximum of seven to ten days.

If refrigerated in a sealed container, dried eggs will keep for one year. Frozen eggs should be kept solidly frozen until needed, then thawed in the refrigerator. Eggs may be frozen at home quite easily, but it is important to use only high-quality fresh eggs. For convenience' sake, freeze eggs in serving-size quantities.

Although egg whites freeze satisfactorily without any additives, frozen whole eggs and egg yolks become lumpy when thawed. To prevent this, add one tablespoon sugar or corn syrup *or* one teaspoon salt to each cup of whole eggs and two tablespoons sugar or corn syrup *or* one teaspoon salt to each cup of egg yolks. Sweetened eggs are suitable for desserts, while salted eggs can be used in main dishes.

To freeze eggs break the eggs into a bowl, separating yolks and whites, if desired. After stirring the eggs to blend (do not beat), strain them through a medium strainer or put them through a food mill. Add sugar or salt, if required, then freeze at 0° or lower in freezer containers leaving sufficient room for expansion. Eggs can be kept frozen for 9 to 12 months.

Basic preparation

There are five basic methods of cooking eggs: scrambling, poaching, soft- or hard-cooking, baking, and frying.

Unlike eggs cooked by the other methods, scrambled eggs are beaten before cooking. How thoroughly they are beaten depends on personal taste. Perfectly scrambled eggs are tender, fluffy, moist, and have a delicate flavor. The secret to perfectly scrambled eggs is simple: do not overcook them. Adding a tablespoon of milk, cream, tomato juice, or other liquid for each egg also makes the scrambled eggs fluffier and more moist.

Basic Scrambled Eggs

Beat 6 eggs, ⅓ cup milk *or* light cream, ¼ to ½ teaspoon salt, and dash pepper with fork. (Mix slightly for eggs with streaks of yellow and white; mix well for a uniform yellow.) Heat 2 tablespoons butter, margarine, *or* bacon fat in skillet till just hot enough to make a drop of water sizzle. Pour in eggs.

Turn heat low. Don't disturb till eggs start to set, then lift and fold over with wide spatula so uncooked part goes to bottom. Avoid breaking up eggs any more than necessary.

Continue cooking till cooked throughout but still glossy and moist, 5 to 8 minutes. Remove from heat immediately. Serves 3 or 4.

Cheese Scrambled Eggs

Cream cheese adds flavor—

Prepare Basic Scrambled Eggs (see recipe, page 833) adding one 3-ounce package cream cheese with chives, cut into pieces, to the seasoned egg-milk mixture. Continue as directed in Basic Scrambled Egg recipe.

Fluffy Scrambled Eggs

Use a double boiler for this version—

Prepare Basic Scrambled Eggs (see recipe, page 833) omitting butter. Cook egg mixture in top of double boiler, stirring with spoon. Water in bottom pan should only simmer and not touch top pan. (Takes twice as long as in skillet.)

Poaching is the cooking method that consists of cooking an egg, broken from its shell, in a liquid. Water is the liquid most commonly used, although milk, cream, consommé, or soup are sometimes used to give the eggs a delicately different flavor. The shape of a poached egg is related to the quality of the egg. Since thin white spreads easily, a high-quality egg (Grade AA or A) with more thick white will give a better shaped poached egg.

If uniformly shaped eggs are desired, use an egg poacher. By the strictest definition, eggs cooked in an egg poacher are not poached since they are cooked above rather than in liquid. Nonetheless, they are still referred to as poached eggs.

Poached Eggs

Add water to a saucepan to depth of 3 to 4 inches; bring just to boiling. Stir simmering water to make a swirl, and slip egg from sauce-dish into middle of the swirl. (Be sure to follow the motion of the swirl with saucedish so egg goes into water in same direction.) Reduce heat to low and cook egg for 3 to 5 minutes, depending on desired doneness. Remove poached egg from water with slotted spoon. Serve immediately on hot buttered toast or English muffin, split and toasted.

One of the easiest ways to prepare eggs is to soft- or hard-cook them. They cook to perfection when the water is kept just below boiling and the cooked eggs are cooled quickly in cold running water.

The term "hard-boiled egg" is a misnomer but was once widely used. The discovery that boiling an egg makes the white tough has led to wide acceptance of the terminology "hard-cooked egg." Tough and rubbery hard-cooked eggs, often with a crumbly yolk, are the result of overcooking or cooking at too high a temperature.

For attractive hard-cooked eggs

To help prevent the harmless, greenish ring that often forms around the yolk of hard-cooked eggs, watch the cooking time carefully and cool the eggs immediately under cold running water.

Soft-Cooked or Hard-Cooked Eggs

Place eggs in saucepan and cover with cold water, at least 1 inch above eggs; rapidly bring to boiling. For *Soft-Cooked Eggs:* Cover pan tightly and remove from heat. Leave eggs in water 2 to 4 minutes, for desired doneness. For more than four eggs, don't turn off heat, but cook, covered, just *below simmering* for 4 to 6 minutes. Promptly cool in cold water.

For *Hard-Cooked Eggs:* When water boils, reduce heat at once to keep water just *below simmering.* Cover and cook eggs for 15 to 20 minutes. Cool immediately in cold water to prevent yolk darkening. To shell hard-cooked eggs, crack shell all over, then roll gently between palms of hands to loosen. Start to peel egg from large end.

The terms baked egg and shirred egg are used interchangeably. These eggs are usually baked in lightly greased individual containers such as muffin tins or custard cups, but they may also be baked on top of a casserole as is traditional with hash. For rich flavor, a little cream or milk may be poured over the unbaked eggs.

Let zesty Brunch Eggs Ranchero make a pleasant eye-opener some morning. Green chilies and tortilla rolls, that replace the usual toast, add a southwestern flavor to this dish.

Shirred (Baked) Eggs

Butter ramekins or custard cups. Break one egg into each; dash with salt and pepper. To *each*, add 1 teaspoon light cream. Set cups in shallow baking pan; pour hot water around them to depth of 1 inch. Bake at 325° till eggs are firm, about 20 minutes.

If desired, after 15 minutes of baking, top each egg with shredded sharp process American cheese. Return eggs to oven and bake till done, 5 to 10 minutes longer.

Frying is the most popular method of egg preparation. Although this method is not recommended nutritionally or from the standpoint of digestibility, thousands of Americans start out their day with an egg fried "sunny-side up" or "over easy." Careful control of the temperature of the fat is important when frying an egg. If the fat or frying pan is too hot, the egg quickly becomes overcooked. A high-quality egg (Grade AA or A) retains its shape better than a Grade B egg when fried.

Fried Eggs

Serve these "sunny-side up" or "over easy"—

In skillet melt a small amount of butter, margarine, *or* bacon fat. Break egg into saucedish; slip egg into skillet. Season with salt and pepper. When the whites are set and edges cooked, add ½ teaspoon water per egg. Cover skillet; cook eggs to desired doneness. If desired, turn egg over with wide spatula; cook briefly.

Besides the basic methods of cooking eggs, several other procedures fall under the classification of basic preparation. When whole eggs are combined with other ingredients, they are usually beaten (whipped until the whites and yolks are blended), either before or after combining them with the other ingredients.

There are various degrees of beating. Recipes usually specify beaten, slightly beaten, or well-beaten eggs. A *slightly beaten egg* is mixed with a fork only till the yolk is broken and there are streaks of white and yellow. *Well-beaten eggs* are beaten until light in color. *Well-beaten egg yolks* look like a thick, lemon-colored foam.

Eggs separate more easily when they are fresh and while they are still cold. The presence of any fat or yolk in the egg white prevents the formation of a stable foam. Therefore, if any yolk gets into the white, carefully remove all of it with the egg shell or the corner of a paper towel.

Egg whites can be whipped to two stages: the soft-peak stage and the stiffly beaten stage. The egg white is beaten to the *soft-peak stage* when the egg white peaks curl slightly. When making a meringue, the whites are beaten to this stage. Then sugar is added gradually while beating the foam to stiff peaks. *Stiffly beaten egg whites* are beaten until peaks stand up straight but are still moist and glossy. Beating past this stage may cause the foam to collapse. Egg whites are also beaten to this stage for angel cakes and soufflés.

Egg whites yield a large volume if allowed to come to room temperature before beating. Adding an acid such as cream of tartar to egg whites before beating stabilizes the beaten foam.

Dried eggs are convenient to have on hand when fresh eggs are not available. To reconstitute dried eggs, sift the egg solids, then measure. Sprinkle the egg over lukewarm water and stir to moisten. Beat until smooth. Once dried eggs have been reconstituted, they should be refrigerated and used within the hour.

In a recipe where eggs are combined with other ingredients, dried eggs need not be reconstituted. Sift with the other dry ingredients, then add the amount of reconstituting liquid to the liquid ingredients. Unless the package indicates that they were dried under rigid bacteriological control, dried eggs should be used only in dishes that are thoroughly cooked.

Uses in cooking

As a cooking ingredient, eggs have three primary functions: coagulation, leavening, and emulsification.

Although eggs coagulate (thicken to a semisoft mass) when cooked by any method, in many dishes this is their primary function. In custards, cakes, cream puffs, cream pie fillings, popovers, and breakfast eggs, the coagulation of the eggs is important in giving structural support. Eggs also bind together other ingredients in dishes such as meat loaf. When foods are dipped into egg before frying, the egg coating coagulates and browns. Eggs are sometimes used to clarify coffee or broth. As the egg thickens, it encloses small particles present in the liquid.

The amount of leavening eggs provide depends on the amount of air beaten into and retained by the eggs. Since egg white can be beaten to a much more stable foam than either egg yolk or whole egg, it is usually beaten separately for use as a leavening. The light, porous texture of food products such as angel food cakes and puffy omelets is achieved by using an egg white foam as the leavening agent.

As an egg white foam is heated, the trapped air expands and the egg coagulates, giving the foam a porous structure.

The third function of the egg in cooking is to emulsify. The classic example of this function is in mayonnaise, although egg also emulsifies cream puffs, ice cream, and hollandaise sauce ingredients. Mayonnaise is made from oil and vinegar, two substances which won't normally combine. The addition of egg yolk, however, enables the oil to stay suspended in the liquid. Egg yolk can act as an emulsifying agent because it forms a thin protein film around the oil droplets that will mix with liquids such as water or vinegar.

In addition to these three functions, eggs are used to add color and flavor to sauces, to prevent the formation of large sugar or ice crystals in candies and sherbets, and when hard-cooked, as an ingredient in or garnish for casseroles, soups, main dishes, and salads.

Using whole eggs: When talking about whole egg cookery, three dishes deserve special mention—custards, plain or French omelets, and cream puffs.

Eggs are a very important ingredient in custard since the mixture is essentially milk thickened by eggs. There are two types of custard, stirred custard and baked custard. Although both have the same ingredients, the egg in stirred custard is coagulated by cooking it on top of the range, while the egg in baked custard is coagulated by baking it in the oven.

When preparing custard, care must be taken to control the cooking temperature accurately. Overcooking results in a curdled stirred custard or a watery baked custard. Stirred custard should be cooked over low heat or over hot water in a double boiler. When baking a custard, set the cups of uncooked custard in a pan of water to equalize the temperature inside and out, thus allowing the custard to cook evenly.

Although some omelets use separated eggs, the plain or French omelet uses whole eggs. There is actually little difference between French omelets and scrambled eggs except that French omelets are stirred less. A perfect plain omelet is tender and moist, yet browned on the bottom. Specially designed omelet pans are available for use, but any shallow skillet with flared sides can be used for omelets.

Eggs perform two functions in cream puffs—emulsification and coagulation. Cream puffs have a high proportion of fat and the eggs help mix this fat with the other ingredients. As the cream puffs bake, the coagulated egg provides much of the cream puff structure.

Cherry Cream Puffs

  1 stick piecrust mix
  2 eggs
  1 21-ounce can cherry pie filling
  1 pint frozen whipped dessert
      topping, thawed
  ½ cup flaked coconut

Crumble piecrust mix into ⅔ cup boiling water; cook and stir vigorously till pastry forms ball and leaves sides of pan. Cook 1 minute over low heat, stirring constantly. Add eggs, one at a time; beat with electric mixer at low speed for 1 minute after each addition.

For *each* cream puff, drop about 3 tablespoons mixture onto greased baking sheet. Bake at 425° for 15 minutes. Reduce temperature to 350°. Continue baking till cream puffs are dry and golden brown, about 20 to 25 minutes. Remove from baking sheet; cool thoroughly.

Cut off tops; remove excess webbing. Set aside ½ *cup* of the pie filling; fold dessert topping and coconut into remaining pie filling. Using about ½ cup cherry mixture for each, fill cream puffs. Replace tops; spoon reserved pie filling over puffs. Makes 8 servings.

Tiny Cream Puffs

In saucepan combine 4 tablespoons butter or margarine and ½ cup water; heat to boiling. Add ½ cup sifted all-purpose flour and dash salt all at once; stir vigorously. Cook, stirring constantly, till mixture pulls away from sides of pan and forms a ball that doesn't separate. Remove from heat; cool slightly. Add 2 eggs, one at a time, beating vigorously after each till smooth. Drop by scant teaspoonfuls 2 inches apart on greased baking pan from toaster oven. (You can do about 1½ dozen at a time.)

Bake at 400° till golden brown, about 20 minutes. Remove from toaster oven; cool on rack. Repeat baking process with remaining dough. At serving time, cut off tops of puffs and fill with seafood or chicken salad, *or* fill with ice cream and top with chocolate sauce. Makes about 4 dozen.

Give deviled eggs a decorative appearance by squeezing the creamy egg yolk filling through a pastry tube.

After mixing the mashed egg yolk with mayonnaise and seasonings, whites can also be refilled with heaping spoonfuls of filling.

In addition to their uses in custards, plain omelets, and cream puffs, whole eggs are also used in innumerable recipes. Although they are most widely used at breakfast, whole eggs are an ingredient in so many main dishes, salads, and desserts that it is easy to include them in the menu for any meal. For brunch, try Easy Eggs A La King or Brunch Eggs Ranchero. Hot Egg Salad Deluxe is an unusual main dish for lunch and delicious Deviled Eggs are just as good for indoor meals as they are for outdoor picnics.

Deviled Eggs

Halve hard-cooked eggs lengthwise; remove yolks and mash with desired combination of seasonings, below. Refill whites.

1. For 6 eggs use ¼ cup mayonnaise, 1 teaspoon vinegar, 1 teaspoon prepared mustard, ⅛ teaspoon salt, and dash pepper.

2. For 5 eggs use 2 tablespoons mayonnaise, 2 tablespoons chopped ripe olives, 2 tablespoons vinegar, 1 teaspoon prepared mustard, and salt and pepper to taste.

3. Other combinations may include: horseradish, anchovies, parsley, chopped onions or chives, flaked seafood, chopped stuffed green olives, crisp-cooked bacon.

Spanish Eggs

A hot egg main dish—

 ½ cup chopped onion
 3 tablespoons butter or margarine
 3 tablespoons all-purpose flour
 2 teaspoons sugar
 1 28-ounce can tomatoes, undrained
 1 small bay leaf
 6 hard-cooked eggs
 ¼ cup mayonnaise
 1 teaspoon prepared mustard
 ¾ cup fine dry bread crumbs
 2 tablespoons butter, melted

Cook onion in the 3 tablespoons butter till tender. Blend in flour, sugar, ¾ teaspoon salt, and dash pepper. Add tomatoes and bay leaf. Cook and stir till thick and bubbly. Remove bay leaf. Pour into 10x6x1¾-inch baking dish.

Halve eggs lengthwise; remove yolks and mash. Mix yolks with mayonnaise, mustard, ⅛ teaspoon salt, and dash pepper; refill egg whites. Arrange in sauce. Combine crumbs and melted butter; sprinkle atop. Bake at 425° for 10 minutes. Serve over buttered noodles or toast, if desired. Serves 6.

Light-as-a-cloud gourmet dish

Be ready to accept compliments when you→ serve Fluffy Cheese Soufflé. Use a collar to let it puff above the baking dish.

Brunch Eggs Ranchero

　　5 slices bacon, cut up
　　1 16-ounce can tomatoes, undrained
　　　　and cut up
　　2 tablespoons chopped green
　　　　chilies (about 2 chilies)
　　1 clove garlic, minced
　　4 eggs
　　　　　•　•　•
　　　　Tortilla Rolls

In skillet cook bacon till crisp; drain off excess fat. Add tomatoes, chilies, and garlic; heat through. Divide among 4 individual bakers. Carefully slip one egg atop tomato mixture in each baker. Season lightly with salt and pepper.

　Bake at 325° till eggs are set, about 20 to 25 minutes. Top each with a crisp bacon curl. Serve with Tortilla Rolls. Makes 4 servings.

　Tortilla Rolls: Heat canned or frozen tortillas in boiling water according to package directions. Spread one side of each with butter. Roll up with butter inside. Place on ovenproof pan. Cover; heat at 325° for 5 to 10 minutes.

Easy Eggs À La King

In saucepan cook ½ cup chopped celery, ¼ cup chopped green pepper, and ¼ cup finely chopped onion in 2 tablespoons cooking oil till tender. Add one 10½-ounce can condensed cream of celery soup, 1 cup diced process American cheese; and ½ cup milk; heat and stir till cheese melts. Add 4 hard-cooked eggs, chopped, and 6 pimiento-stuffed green olives, sliced; heat through. Spoon over hot buttered toast. Trim with hard-cooked egg slices. Serves 4.

Hot Egg Salad Deluxe

Prepare 1½ cups finely crushed saltine cracker crumbs. Blend together *1 cup* of the crumbs; 6 hard-cooked eggs, chopped; 1 cup mayonnaise or salad dressing; 3 slices bacon, crisp-cooked and crumbled; ½ cup diced celery; 2 tablespoons diced canned pimiento; ¼ cup milk; ¼ teaspoon salt; and dash pepper. Turn into 9-inch pie plate. Blend remaining crumbs with 2 tablespoons butter or margarine, melted; sprinkle over casserole. Bake at 400° till golden, about 25 minutes. Makes 4 servings.

Using separated eggs: Although packaged in a common container, the egg yolk and egg white have widely different properties. Thus, the egg is often separated and the yolk used as an emulsifier or thickener, while the beaten egg white is used as a leavening agent. This enables the cook to prepare dishes that are very different from those using whole eggs.

　Cream pie filling and hollandaise sauce, as well as mayonnaise which was discussed above, are dishes that use the egg yolk as one of their basic ingredients.

For a high, fluffy meringue, beat the room-temperature egg whites with vanilla and cream of tartar to the soft-peak stage.

While gradually adding sugar, continue beating till egg whites are stiffly beaten and sugar is all dissolved (test with fingers).

Cooked Mustard Sauce

In small saucepan combine 2 beaten egg yolks, ¼ cup water, 2 tablespoons prepared mustard, 2 tablespoons vinegar, 1 tablespoon sugar, and 1 teaspoon seasoned salt. Cook over low heat, stirring constantly, till mixture is thickened, about 5 minutes. Remove from heat. Blend in 1 tablespoon garlic spread. Cool mixture thoroughly. Whip ½ cup whipping cream; fold into cooled mixture. Makes 1⅓ cups.

Classic examples of the use of egg whites are meringue and angel food cake. In both of these, the egg white foam is the only leavening. Therefore, top-quality egg whites beaten to a stiff but not dry foam are vital for a satisfactory product.

Mint Patty Alaskas

Beat 2 egg whites with ¼ teaspoon cream of tartar, ¼ teaspoon vanilla, and dash salt to soft peaks. Gradually add ¼ cup sugar, beating to stiff peaks. Place 2 sponge cake dessert cups on cutting board; top *each* with a chocolate-coated peppermint ice cream patty.

Cover with meringue, spreading thicker over ice cream and thinner around cake; seal edges at bottom. Sprinkle meringue with 1 tablespoon crushed peppermint-stick candy. Bake at 500° till meringue is browned, about 2 to 3 minutes. Serve at once. Makes 2 servings.

By separating the eggs and then using both the yolks and the whites in a recipe, the cook is able to get leavening from the egg white foam as well as the whole egg's flavor and color.

A sponge cake is a foamy cake quite similar to an angel food cake, the basic difference stemming from the use of egg yolk. In a sponge cake the egg yolk adds the color and flavor. Although a sponge cake can be made using only egg yolks, both yolks and whites are used. As with an angel cake, the egg whites are the only leavening. As whenever working with an egg white foam, maximum volume is attained by quickly and carefully folding the other ingredients into the beaten egg whites.

Crushed peppermint candy tops these Mint Patty Alaskas. The soft meringue covers sponge cake and peppermint ice cream.

Cream pie fillings are thickened with both egg, usually only the yolk, and starch. Since starch thickens at a higher temperature and requires a longer cooking time than egg, the starch-liquid mixture of the filling is cooked till thickened before the egg is added. If the egg were added directly to the hot starch-liquid mixture, it would coagulate immediately into small lumps. Therefore, a small amount of the hot mixture is combined with the egg, and then this mixture is stirred into the remaining portion of the hot mixture.

Hollandaise sauce, the classic accompaniment to asparagus, is made from egg yolk, butter, and lemon juice. As in mayonnaise, the egg yolk acts as an emulsifier, but in the hollandaise sauce and the mustard sauce given below it has an additional function—the egg yolk coagulates and thickens the sauce.

Although the ingredients for a puffy omelet are the same as for a plain omelet, different mixing methods result in different products. When making a puffy omelet, the well-beaten egg yolks are folded into the stiffly beaten egg whites. This mixing method produces a large amount of air to make the texture light and puffy.

Sour Cream Omelet

Beat 5 egg yolks till thick and lemon-colored, about 5 minutes; beat in ½ cup dairy sour cream, and ½ teaspoon salt. Fold in 5 stiffly beaten egg whites. Melt 2 tablespoons butter or margarine in a 10-inch ovenproof skillet; pour in egg mixture, leveling gently.

Cook egg mixture over *very low* heat till lightly browned on bottom, about 8 to 10 minutes. Finish cooking at 325° till top is golden brown, 12 to 15 minutes. Loosen; slide omelet onto warm platter. Top with ½ cup dairy sour cream and fresh strawberries. To serve, break in wedges with two forks. Makes 3 to 4 servings.

A soufflé is similar to a puffy omelet except it uses a thick white sauce in combination with the egg yolks. The addition of chopped meat or fish (often leftovers) or shredded cheese turns the soufflé into an elegant main dish. If a dessert soufflé is desired, add sugar and puréed fruit or a flavoring such as chocolate or vanilla.

A soufflé should be baked in an ungreased, straight-sided baking dish to allow the soufflé to rise by clinging to the sides of the dish. As when baking a custard, set the soufflé in a pan of water to permit even cooking.

The fallen soufflé has been used so often as an example of cooking failure that many cooks are afraid to try making a soufflé. Although all soufflés shrink a certain amount as they cool, underbaking is the

An elegant brunch omelet

←Sour cream adds tangy flavor to Sour Cream Omelet. Next time, top with plump fresh blueberries instead of strawberries.

cause of their rapid collapse. To prevent this, watch the baking time and temperature carefully and serve a soufflé as soon as it comes from the oven. This is one time when the guests can wait for the food but the food will not wait for the guests.

Fluffy Cheese Soufflé

  6 tablespoons butter or margarine
  ⅓ cup all-purpose flour
  ½ teaspoon salt
    Dash cayenne
  1½ cups milk
  12 ounces sharp natural Cheddar cheese, shredded or diced
  6 egg yolks
  6 stiffly beaten egg whites

Melt butter; blend in flour and seasonings. Add milk all at once. Cook and stir over medium heat till thickened and bubbly. Remove from heat. Add cheese; stir till cheese melts.

Beat egg yolks till thick and lemon-colored. Slowly add cheese mixture, stirring constantly. Cool slightly. Gradually pour over beaten egg whites, folding in thoroughly. Pour into *ungreased* 2-quart soufflé dish.

Attach a "collar" to the soufflé dish for a high soufflé: Measure enough foil or waxed paper to go around casserole plus a 2- to 3-inch overlap. Fold foil in thirds, lengthwise. Lightly butter one side. Letting collar extend 2 inches above top of casserole, fasten with pins around the dish (buttered side in).

Bake at 300° till knife inserted halfway between center and edge comes out clean, about 1½ hours. Gently peel off collar and serve immediately. Makes 6 to 8 servings.

As can be seen, the egg is a versatile food that can contribute to the color, flavor, and nutritive value of any meal. In the United States, breakfast often is a tasty plate of fried eggs, a boiled or poached egg, or a scrambled egg. At lunch or brunch, an omelet, soufflé, egg sandwich, egg casserole, or eggs Benedict makes a tasty entrée. Even at company dinners, eggs can be one of the major ingredients in the angel food cake, popovers, molded aspic, or dessert soufflé.

EGG BEATER—A hand-operated rotary beater used to whip eggs as well as other liquid or semiliquid mixtures.

EGG COOKER—An electrical appliance or top-of-the-range utensil designed to poach or cook eggs in the shell.

EGGNOG—A beverage, similar in ingredients to stirred custard, made of eggs, milk, sugar, and flavoring. The name is thought to have been coined because the egg-milk mixture was served in a noggin, a small mug with an upright handle.

Eggnog, often flavored with sherry, rum, brandy, whiskey, or wine, has become a traditional Christmas drink. Because of its protein value, eggnog is served throughout the year to invalids and people with digestive problems. (See also *Beverage*.)

Instant Nog

Starts with an instant pudding mix—

> 1   3¾-ounce package *instant* vanilla pudding mix
> ⅓ cup sugar
> 1   teaspoon vanilla
> 6   cups milk
> 2   egg yolks
> 2   stiffly beaten egg whites
>   Ground nutmeg

In a large mixing bowl beat together the vanilla pudding mix, sugar, vanilla, milk, and egg yolks. Carefully fold in the stiffly beaten egg whites. Chill thoroughly. Pour into punch cups or glasses and top with a dash of nutmeg. Makes about 8 cups.

Coffee Royal Eggnog

Delicately flavored with instant coffee powder—

Combine 4 cups dairy *or* canned eggnog, well chilled; 1 pint vanilla ice cream, softened; 2 to 3 teaspoons instant coffee powder; and ½ teaspoon rum flavoring. Blend thoroughly. Pour into punch bowl or chilled cups; top with dollops of whipped cream and dash of ground nutmeg. Makes 10 to 12 servings.

Guests return for seconds when the holiday beverage is Coffee Royal Eggnog. Float large dollops of whipped cream for garnish.

Festive Freeze

> ¼ cup sugar
> 2   tablespoons all-purpose flour
> ¼ teaspoon salt
> 2   cups milk
> 2   well-beaten egg yolks
> 2   cups dairy eggnog
> 1½ teaspoons vanilla
>
> •   •   •
>
> 2   egg whites
> ¼ cup sugar

In saucepan combine the first ¼ cup sugar, flour, and salt. Gradually stir in milk. Cook, stirring constantly, till thickened. Stir small amount of hot mixture into egg yolks, return to hot mixture. Cook and stir 2 minutes more. Stir in dairy eggnog and vanilla.

Pour eggnog mixture into refrigerator tray and freeze till soft ice crystals form around edges. Turn into chilled mixing bowl and beat with electric or rotary beater till smooth and fluffy. Beat egg whites till soft peaks form; gradually add remaining sugar, beating to stiff peaks. Quickly fold meringue into eggnog mixture. Return to refrigerator tray; freeze till firm. Makes 6 to 8 servings.

Eggnog

⅓ cup sugar
2 egg yolks
4 cups milk
2 egg whites
3 tablespoons sugar
1 teaspoon vanilla
  Brandy *or* rum flavoring to
    taste
½ cup whipping cream, whipped
  Ground nutmeg

Beat the ⅓ cup sugar into egg yolks. Add ¼ teaspoon salt; stir in milk. Cook and stir over medium heat till mixture coats metal spoon; cool. Beat egg whites till foamy. Gradually add the 3 tablespoons sugar, beating to soft peaks. Add to custard and mix well. Add vanilla and flavoring. Chill 3 or 4 hours. Pour into punch bowl. Top with dollops of whipped cream; dash with nutmeg. Serves 6 to 8.

Use a sharp knife to cut homemade noodles the desired width. Make the noodles ahead, then store in plastic bag till ready to use.

EGG NOODLE—Pasta made with whole eggs or egg yolks. After cutting in strips ranging from 1/16 of an inch to several inches wide, the noodles are dried. Noodles are about the only pasta that homemakers can make at home. (See also *Noodle*.)

Parsley-Buttered Noodles

1 beaten egg
2 tablespoons milk
½ teaspoon salt
1 cup sifted all-purpose flour
2 tablespoons butter or margarine
2 tablespoons snipped parsley

In medium bowl combine egg, milk, and salt. Add enough of the flour to make a stiff dough. Roll very thin on floured surface; let stand 20 minutes. Roll up loosely; slice into noodles ¼ inch wide. Spread out and let dry 2 hours. Place in clear plastic bag and store.

To cook, drop noodles into boiling, salted water. Cook, uncovered, for about 10 minutes. Drain. Add butter or margarine and parsley. Toss to mix well. Makes 6 servings.

EGG POACHER—A covered saucepan with an inset that has individual cups to hold eggs. Eggs dropped into the buttered cups hold their shape as they steam to the desired doneness.

EGG POACHING RING—A metal ring with handle that confines an egg to the ring's shape while it is poaching.

EGG SAUCE—Any sauce that contains egg, specifically chopped hard-cooked eggs, in a thickened cream sauce.

Creamy Egg Sauce

2 tablespoons butter or margarine
2 tablespoons all-purpose flour
1 cup milk
1 hard-cooked egg, chopped

Melt butter; blend in flour, ¼ teaspoon salt, and dash white pepper. Add milk. Cook and stir till thick and bubbly. Add egg.

Egg wedger, at left, works like scissors to cut hard-cooked egg in even wedges. Egg slicer, right, separates egg into slices.

EGG SLICER—A metal or plastic kitchen utensil with fine steel wires used to slice hard-cooked eggs. The egg is placed in the aluminum or plastic holder, and a hinged rack of evenly spaced thin wires is lowered over it, cutting the egg into even, separate wedges or slices. The sliced egg can then be used as a colorful garnish for tossed salads and vegetables or in creamed dishes.

Another utensil which works somewhat the same way, called an egg wedger, cuts a hard-cooked egg into 6 even wedges.

EGGPLANT—A purple or white pear-shaped fruit used as a vegetable. Possibly of oriental origin, the eggplant was first written about in a fifth century Chinese book. It was thought to cause insanity and so was called the "mad apple."

In the 1800s, the dark purple vegetable was used solely for table decoration and ornamentation until it was found to be safe for consumption. Today, eggplant is popular in Europe and America because of its unique eating qualities.

Also called egg fruit, aubergine, and guinea squash, the vegetable was named eggplant because the first varieties were about the size of eggs.

How eggplant is produced: Eggplant grows on a tall plant which bears woolly green leaves and purple flowers. In America, the plant is cultivated chiefly in the tropical Florida and Gulf Coast areas.

Nutritional value: Uncooked eggplant is low in calories and contains fair amounts of vitamin C, the B vitamins, and some vitamin A. However, cooked eggplant is valued for its flavor and texture rather than for its nutritional contribution.

Types of eggplant: The color of eggplant, ranging from white to yellow and violet to purple, depends on the variety. Purple eggplants are the most common variety found and used in the United States.

The shape of the vegetable varies from the familiar egg or pear-shaped form to round, oblong, and oval horticultural varieties. The long, narrow, snake eggplant and the small, smooth dwarf eggplant are examples of its diverse shapes.

How to select: Select an eggplant with a dark, shiny, smooth skin. Dark spots indicate decay, so choose one that is firm and heavy. One medium-size eggplant (about 1 pound) constitutes about four servings. Although most plentiful in August and September, eggplants are available in supermarkets throughout the year.

How to store: Store eggplants in a cool, humid place. Raw eggplant can be stored in the refrigerator for up to two weeks, while the maximum storage time for cooked eggplant is four or five days.

How to prepare: Eggplant can be peeled or the skin can be left on to hold the tender pulp together during cooking. Boiling eggplant in water removes its unique vegetable flavor, so use the French or Italian technique of baking the eggplant in skin or stewing in oil or broth. A well-cooked eggplant exhibits a crusty exterior and a moist, tender inside.

Dip eggplant slices in flour and milk mixture and deep-fat fry them. Top scalloped eggplant with cheese, mushrooms, or sour cream. Cube eggplant and combine with favorite meat chunks for kabobs.

Stuff hollowed-out eggplant with ground meat and bake. Broil thick slices of eggplant brushed with butter and seasoning and serve as a second vegetable.

How to use: Serve eggplant appetizers and hors d'oeuvres at company meals. Try a new casserole or salad with eggplant dices for the family. This versatile vegetable is delicious prepared with cheese sauces and served with favorite lamb or chicken dinners. (See also *Vegetable*.)

Pan–Fried Eggplant

Peel 1 medium eggplant (1½ pounds). Cut in half lengthwise, then cut crosswise making ½-inch slices. Combine 1 slightly beaten egg and 1 tablespoon cold water. Dip eggplant in egg mixture, then in mixture of ½ cup fine dry bread crumbs, ½ teaspoon salt, and dash pepper. Fry in hot oil till tender and brown, about 2 to 3 minutes on each side. Drain on paper toweling. Sprinkle lightly with salt. Keep warm. Makes 4 to 6 servings.

The intriguing eggplant, a distant relative of the potato, is a fruit used as a vegetable. The smooth, glossy, purple-skinned variety is popular in the United States as a table vegetable.

Eggplant-Cheese Stacks, fried seasoned stacks of eggplant and cheese slices, are served as a vegetable or main dish.

Eggplant Skillet

Sprinkle cheese over beef and eggplant dish—

1 pound ground beef
¼ cup chopped onion
¼ cup chopped celery
1 8-ounce can tomato sauce (1 cup)
½ cup water
½ to ¾ teaspoon dried oregano leaves, crushed
½ to ¾ teaspoon chili powder
1 small eggplant, cut in ½-inch slices (1 pound)
4 ounces sharp process American cheese, shredded (1 cup)
Paprika
Shredded Parmesan cheese

Cook beef, onion, and celery till meat is browned. Drain off excess fat. Stir in tomato sauce, water, oregano, and chili powder. Season eggplant slices with salt and pepper. Arrange on top of meat sauce. Cover and simmer till eggplant is tender, about 15 to 20 minutes. Top with shredded process American cheese and sprinkle with paprika. Serve with Parmesan cheese. Makes 4 or 5 servings.

Eggplant-Cheese Stacks

1 medium eggplant (1½ pounds)
4 or 5 slices sharp process American cheese
1 slightly beaten egg
¼ cup milk
1 2⅜-ounce package seasoned coating mix for chicken
3 tablespoons salad oil

Peel eggplant and cut into eight or ten ½-inch slices. Cook slices, covered, in small amount of boiling water for 2 to 3 minutes; drain well. Place a slice of cheese between each 2 slices of eggplant; trim cheese to fit. Combine egg and milk. Dip both sides of eggplant stacks in egg mixture, then in coating mix. Cook in hot oil till golden brown, about 5 to 6 minutes on each side. Serves 4 or 5.

Elegant Eggplant

Peel and thinly slice 1 large eggplant (1¾ pounds). Dip into 2 well-beaten eggs, then in 1½ cups finely crushed saltine crackers (about 42 crackers). Brown eggplant slices slowly in a little hot shortening. Place *one-fourth* of the eggplant slices in bottom of 2-quart casserole; top with *one-fourth* of one 8-ounce package sliced sharp process American cheese.

Combine two 8-ounce cans tomato sauce (2 cups), ½ teaspoon Worcestershire sauce, and 1 teaspoon dried oregano leaves, crushed. Spoon *one-fourth* of the sauce (about ½ cup) over cheese. Repeat layers till all ingredients are used, ending with sauce. Cover and bake at 350° till eggplant is tender, about 50 to 60 minutes. Snip parsley over top. Serves 8.

Italian Eggplant

Peel and cut 1 medium eggplant (1½ pounds) into ½-inch slices. Dip into ½ cup butter or margarine, melted; then into mixture of ¾ cup fine dry bread crumbs and ¼ teaspoon salt. Put on greased baking sheet. Spoon one 8- or 10¾-ounce can spaghetti sauce with mushrooms atop slices. Sprinkle with 1 tablespoon dried oregano leaves, crushed; and 1 cup shredded mozzarella cheese. Bake at 450° for 10 to 12 minutes. Serves 4 or 5.

Crisp corn chips circle around the tasty eggplant and vegetable dish, Eggplant Crunch Casserole, to add texture and flavor.

Baked Eggplant

Serve eggplant for a new and different baked vegetable with a favorite meal—

    1 medium eggplant
 ½ cup salad oil
    1 clove garlic, crushed
    2 tablespoons snipped parsley
      Crushed oregano leaves
      Salt
      Freshly ground pepper

• • •

    2 medium tomatoes, cut in ½-inch
      slices
      Grated Parmesan cheese

Cut eggplant in half lengthwise and place in greased, shallow baking dish. Combine oil and garlic; brush *half* over cut surfaces. Sprinkle with parsley and oregano. Season with salt and pepper. Top eggplant with tomato slices; drizzle with remaining oil mixture. Sprinkle with oregano, salt, and pepper.

Bake, uncovered, at 400° till eggplant is tender, about 45 to 60 minutes. Sprinkle eggplant with additional snipped parsley before serving, if desired. Pass bowl of grated Parmesan cheese. Makes 6 servings.

Eggplant Crunch Casserole

    1 small eggplant, peeled and
      cubed (1 pound)

• • •

    1 cup chopped celery
 ½ cup chopped onion
 ½ cup chopped green pepper
 ¼ cup butter or margarine

• • •

    1 8-ounce can tomato sauce
    4 ounces sharp process American
      cheese, shredded (1 cup)
 1½ cups coarsely crushed corn
      chips

In large skillet or saucepan cook eggplant, celery, onion, and green pepper in butter or margarine till tender, about 15 minutes. Stir in tomato sauce, cheese, and *1 cup* of the crushed corn chips. Turn into 1½-quart casserole. Bake, covered, at 350° till heated through, about 25 to 30 minutes. Before serving, wreathe casserole with the remaining ½ cup corn chips. Makes 6 to 8 servings.

Scalloped Eggplant

    1 large eggplant, diced (4 cups)

• • •

 ⅓ cup milk
    1 10½-ounce can condensed cream
      of mushroom soup
    1 slightly beaten egg
 ½ cup chopped onion
 ¾ cup packaged herb-seasoned
      stuffing mix

• • •

      Cheese Topper

Cook diced eggplant in boiling salted water till tender, 6 to 7 minutes; drain. Meanwhile, gradually stir milk into soup; blend in egg. Add drained eggplant, onion, and stuffing; toss lightly to mix. Turn into greased 10x6x1¾-inch baking dish.

For *Cheese Topper*, finely crush ½ cup packaged herb-seasoned stuffing mix; toss with 2 tablespoons melted butter or margarine. Sprinkle over casserole. Top casserole with 4 ounces sharp process American cheese, shredded (1 cup). Bake at 350° till hot, about 20 minutes. Makes 6 to 8 servings.

EGGS BENEDICT—Distinctive egg dish consisting of a toasted English muffin or bread spread with butter and topped with a ham slice and poached egg served with a hollandaise, cheese, or white sauce. This classic recipe, popular for breakfast and weekend brunches, is occasionally garnished with truffle and tomatoes or parsley.

Eggs Benedict

For each serving toast an English muffin half. Top each half with a thin slice of broiled ham and a soft-poached egg. Ladle Blender Hollandaise over the egg and sprinkle with paprika. Garnish with truffle slices and grilled tomato wedges, if desired. Serve immediately while hot.

For *Blender Hollandaise:* In blender place 3 egg yolks, 1 tablespoon lemon juice, and dash cayenne. Cover; quickly turn blender on and off. Heat ½ cup butter or margarine till melted and bubbling hot. Turn blender on high speed; slowly pour butter or margarine into egg mixture, blending till thick and fluffy, about 30 seconds. Makes about ⅔ cup sauce.

ELDERBERRY—The dark purple or red berry fruit of the elder bush, a member of the honeysuckle family. The berries, found growing in large clusters on the bushes, are used for jams, jellies, and homemade wines. Elderberries freeze well and can be dried. (See also *Berry*.)

ELECTION CAKE—A yeast-raised loaf cake flavored with fruits, spices, and liquor. Originating during the eighteenth century in Hartford, Connecticut, the highly seasoned cake was often served at town meetings. It soon became known as the Hartford Election Cake. Frugal Colonial homemakers made this cake by combining leftover bread dough with additional spices, fruits, and liquors. One of the first foods to

Classic brunch idea

Top a toasted English muffin with a ham slice and a poached egg. Spoon Blender Hollandaise over Eggs Benedict and garnish.

be associated with politics, election cake is now used as a coffee bread or dessert.

ELECTRIC PORTABLE APPLIANCE—Electric kitchen helpers that produce heat or turn motors by means of electricity to make the homemaker's work easier and faster. Some of the heating appliances available are toasters, waffle bakers, broilers, coffee makers, hot plates, corn poppers, frypans, roasters, griddles, deep-fat fryers, and rotisseries. Motor-driven portable electric appliances include appliances such as food mixers, ice crushers, can openers, juice extractors, blenders, and electric kitchen clocks and timers.

Consider family and personal needs and uses when buying a small electric appliance. Select the best size to fit family needs. Check construction and important features such as the materials it's made of, lid and feet positions, signal lights, attachments, and the Underwriters' Laboratories mark of approval.

The appliance should have a pleasing appearance, be easy to clean and store, possess an adequate guarantee, and be easily repaired and serviced by a competent serviceman. In all cases, the instruction booklet accompanying the portable electric appliance should be read very carefully and saved for future reference.

ELECTRONIC COOKERY—Roasting and baking in a specialized oven which employs high frequency microwaves to cook food in a fraction of standard times. As the microwave energy penetrates, molecules within the food vibrate against each other producing the heat which does the cooking. (See also *Microwave Cookery*.)

ELK—A large member of the deer family. The elk is hunted seasonally in such northwestern states as Colorado, Idaho, Montana, Oregon, and Washington in accordance with local game laws and animal supply. The nourishing rich meat can be prepared like beef with a slow cooking process. (See also *Game*.)

EMMENTHALER   *(em′ uhn tä′ ler)*—The name for natural Swiss cheese developed in the Emmental Valley of Switzerland.

Many types of Swiss are made under other names. A high quality cow's milk is needed to produce Swiss, making it one of the most difficult cheeses to make. The sweet-flavored cheese is excellent for cheese dishes and toppings. (See also *Cheese*.)

EMPANADA *(em′ puh nä′ duh)*—A Mexican meat pie or turnover made from cheese, meat or fish, and a vegetable filling. In South America, empanadas are eaten as sandwiches and are sold on street corners. (See also *Mexican Cookery*.)

Empanadas

```
1 teaspoon butter or margarine
¼ pound ground beef
2 tablespoons finely chopped
    onion
2 tablespoons chopped green
    pepper
½ cup finely chopped canned
    pears
½ cup finely chopped canned
    peaches
½ cup chopped tomatoes
⅛ to ¼ teaspoon ground cinnamon
    Crust
1 beaten egg
```

Melt butter. Cook ground beef, onion, and green pepper till tender. Stir in fruits, tomatoes, cinnamon, and ¼ teaspoon salt. Cover; simmer 5 minutes. Drain. Makes 1¼ cups.

Crust: Sift together 1½ cups sifted all-purpose flour, 1 tablespoon sugar, and ¼ teaspoon salt. Cut in ½ cup shortening. Add 1 beaten egg yolk and ¼ cup milk; mix. Turn out on board and knead about 1 minute. Roll to ⅛-inch thickness. Cut in 5½-inch rounds.

Place filling on one half of dough round; moisten edge. Cover filling with remaining half of round; pinch together. Prick top. Place dough on lightly greased baking sheet. Brush tops with beaten egg. Bake at 400° for 12 to 15 minutes. Makes 5 servings.

EMULSION—A mixture of two liquid ingredients which do not dissolve into each other. One liquid is suspended in the second liquid as tiny globules.

Examples of emulsions include oil and vinegar in French salad dressing, and milk and fat in buttermilk. An oil or butter and egg yolk emulsion gives mayonnaise or hollandaise sauce its consistency.

ENCHILADA *(en' chuh lä' da, -lad' uh)* —A Mexican tortilla cooked and filled with meat and vegetables or cheese combinations and topped with spicy chili and tomato sauce or grated cheese. Baked enchiladas can be stuffed with chicken, fish, seafood, or meat with different vegetables. Enchiladas are especially popular in the Pacific Coast states and in Texas, New Orleans, Louisiana, and California. (See also *Mexican Cookery*.)

Cheese Enchiladas

Thoroughly wash 1 pound dried whole red chilies or 6 ounces (about 3⅓ cups) dried, seeded red chilies. If not already seeded, stem chilies, slit, and remove seed veins and seeds. Wash again. Cover with cold water; bring to vigorous boil. Drain and wash again. Put chilies through food chopper, then through a sieve. Stir in 1 clove garlic, crushed; ¼ teaspoon dried oregano leaves, crushed; pinch ground comino (cumin seed); and ¼ cup salad oil. To one 10½-ounce can condensed beef broth or 1¼

Fry one tortilla at a time on both sides. Use a tongs to quickly turn the tortilla, cooking it only till puffy, not browned.

cups bouillon, add water to make 2¾ cups; add to chili mixture and simmer for 20 minutes. Add salt to the chili mixture to taste.

Heat ½ cup salad oil in a skillet, and when hot, fry 8 tortillas, one at a time, on both sides. (Fry only till they puff a bit, but don't crisp or brown.) After each tortilla is fried, dip it into the hot chili mixture, then place on a platter.

Have ready 12 ounces sharp natural Cheddar cheese, shredded (3 cups); 1 medium onion, finely chopped; and ½ cup chopped pitted ripe olives. *Reserve 1 cup* of the cheese. Place a handful of cheese (about ¼ cup) on each tortilla and sprinkle with onion and olives. Roll up each tortilla and place in greased, shallow baking pan. (At this time the tortillas have become enchiladas, and they may be kept in readiness for baking at this stage.)

Half an hour before serving time, pour rest of the chili mixture over enchiladas; sprinkle with reserved 1 cup cheese. Bake at 350° for 25 minutes. Makes 8 servings. Tortillas are also available frozen or canned.

ENDIVE *(en' dīv, än' dēv)* —A salad green related to the chicory family. The early European colonists brought the sharp-flavored plants to the United States. Endive seed is planted to produce the green. Related to endive is the tightly packed Belgian or French endive. Delicately fringed and curly, endive provides a strong contrast to the broad-leaved escarole which is also a relative to endive. Besides being used as a salad green ingredient, endive is delicious prepared as a vegetable and served with a sauce. (See also *Vegetable*.)

Endive-Avocado Salad

Chill 8 French endives in ice water to crisp. Dry gently with paper toweling. Remove a few outer leaves and set aside. Cut endive stalks into large crosswise slices. In salad bowl combine endive slices; 1 avocado, halved, peeled, and sliced; and 4 scallions *or* green onions, chopped. Season to taste with salt and pepper.

Combine ¼ cup salad oil and 1 tablespoon wine vinegar; pour over endive mixture and toss lightly. Top with 2 tablespoons snipped parsley. Arrange reserved endive leaves around edge of bowl. Serves 6.

ENGLISH COOKERY—Toad in the hole, kippers, bangers 'n mash, shepherd's pie, bubble and squeak. These evocative names do not belong to gourmet fare, but they rather are names of simple English dishes: sausages in batter, salted herring, sausage and mashed potatoes, minced meat cooked in potatoes, and fried potatoes and cabbage, respectively.

This, after all, is English cookery—simply prepared foods that are noted for their heartiness and home-style flavor. English food has been drawn from a mingling of recipes and techniques introduced by successive invaders who, generally influenced a different section of the country.

Under Roman domination, the earliest English tribes were exposed to civilized dining. But, with the subsequent fall of the Roman Empire and the conquest of England by barbaric peoples, these culinary advances virtually disappeared.

Even though they were less cultured than the Romans, the Germanic invaders of the fifth century, who were known as Anglo-Saxons, are credited with establishing hearty foods as the basis for the national cuisine. From their homeland, they brought the arts of baking, brewing, making butter and cheese, and raising livestock. They utilized the food of the land by hunting wild boars, partridges, and rabbits, catching fish, and picking wild berries. And by the eleventh century, the Anglo-Saxons' love of lavish meals and incessant feasting had resulted in the evolution of new ways with food.

The conquering Normans abruptly altered the Anglo-Saxon's food culture. The imaginative Normans prepared refined bread products as well as pastries and meat pies. Foods were seasoned with exotic spices such as ginger, cloves, nutmeg, and cinnamon. To replace the Anglo-Saxon's conglomerate meals, the Normans served dinners in a series of courses.

Internal changes rather than external influences marked the fourteenth-through sixteenth-century advances. Many basic fruit and vegetable varieties were introduced and salads were promoted. In addition, housewives were offered the first cook book written by an English author, *The Boke of Cookery*.

The growing acceptance of sweets, which developed during the Elizabethan Age (1558-1603) was the most notable cuisine change of this period. Queen Elizabeth I became so fond of sweets that she would often excuse herself from the royal dining table to eat sweets she had hidden in her room. A myriad of dishes including cakes, pastries, custards, and jellies were popularized—so much so, in fact, that sweets were soon being served at the beginning of, between, and after meals.

Foreign cooking influences were revived in England during the following centuries. As a mark of respect to William of Orange, Patrick Lamb, who had headed the royal kitchens of England for over 50 years, introduced Dutch cooking methods to England in 1710 with his book, *Royal Cookery*. With increased communication between the American colonies, "all-American" dishes became well known. French cuisine so attracted wealthy Englishmen that they began importing French chefs.

A large portion of the English population, however, did not readily accept French cooking. The English claimed to be better cooks than the French (a claim that is still made) and attempted to prove their superiority by producing more cook books than any other nation. For nearly 100 years, all French cookery was obliterated from English texts.

In the late 1700s this rivalry subsided. And in a unique turnabout, a native Frenchmen, Alexis Soyer, became the most renowned English chef and cook book author of the nineteenth century.

Most of the typically English recipes of today are modernized versions of the inherited dishes. Each generation has adapted the old ideas to incorporate current ingredients and techniques.

Characteristics of English cookery: English dishes are consistently substantial in nature and are planned for use in a well-defined meal pattern.

Christmas dinner is a typical example of how hearty English foods make a substantial meal. Just reading Charles Dickens' *A Christmas Carol* brings a mouth-watering picture to the imagination. Although today a turkey may replace the

Cratchit's roasted goose, the enormity of the meal remains the same. Everyone is expected to take at least second and sometimes third helpings of golden brown roast turkey, sage and onion stuffing, baked or fluffy mashed potatoes, steaming gravy, and applesauce. This is followed by a blazing plum pudding with hard sauce, tiny mince pies, jellies (gelatin), custards, and an assortment of confections.

Common to all of England is a wide array of meats. Although often called "a nation of beef-eaters," mutton, venison, veal, lamb, and ham are also popular for roasts, chops, meat pies, and stews. Suckling pig, boar's head, and large and small game such as Cornish game hens are served at meals celebrating special occasions.

Since England is an island, fish and seafood are among the most abundant and favorite foods. Interestingly, however, pagan Britains did not eat fish, but used it in sacrifices to their gods. Fresh fish are available daily in most areas of England. Shops specializing in newspaper-wrapped fish and chips (batter-fried fish and deep-fat fried potato strips) abound. Oysters, prawns, sole, and salmon are plentiful. Herring are lightly salted and briefly smoked (bloaters) or more liberally salted and heavily smoked (kippers).

Of the traditional English meal pattern —hearty breakfast, moderate lunch, late afternoon tea, and course-by-course dinner —the style of breakfast and teatime are the most unique to this cuisine.

Although the current trend is toward a hurried breakfast of tea and toast, the English are long-remembered for their large breakfasts. The upper-classes breakfasted buffet-style with oatmeal porridge (more recently cornflakes), bacon, eggs, fried bread, hot toast with marmalade, and large quantities of hot tea. Fish, fruit, fried mushrooms, or grilled tomatoes were sometimes included. The lower-classes were not so lavish but still made the first meal of the day a large one: hot porridge, kippers, fried bread, lashings of marmalade (usually orange) and toast, and mugs of hot, scalding tea (with sugar and milk).

England's worldwide culinary fame is closely linked with tea, a term that denotes both the nation's favorite beverage and a meal as well. Introduction of this beverage to England is credited to seventeenth-century Dutchmen who brought tea back with them from East Indian trading posts. However, just when tea took on the added meaning of a meal is not clear. The Duchess of Bedford is said to have introduced the afternoon tea to dispel a five o'clock "sinking feeling."

The meal called tea has two different connotations which depend on whether it is served during the week or on weekends. During week days, tea is similar to the American habit of drinking a cup of coffee in the late afternoon, except that the British have a cup of tea with a bun or small cake. On weekends, tea, with the possible inclusion of dainty sandwiches of watercress, or shrimp, ham, thinly sliced cucumber, and tomatoes; cookies, crumpets; lemon-filled tarts; Scottish scones with jam and cream; an assortment of cakes and small sweet rolls; or platters filled with sausage rolls and slices of pork pie, takes the place of a full evening meal.

One of the most typical weekend teas consists of pork pie, lettuce, celery sticks, bread and butter, possibly jam (preserves), cake, and a pot of tea. This style of dining probably came about because the British often entertained company by having a meal on Sunday afternoon.

Regional English cookery: The groups of people that established homes in England tended to concentrate in certain regions of the country: Normans in the north, Celts in the southwest, and Anglo-Saxons in the southeast. Many of the well-known recipes are still primarily prepared in the region of their origin, but others such as steak and kidney pie and plum pudding have become so naturalized to the English cuisine as a whole that their origin has been somewhat obscured. Yorkshire pudding (a popoverlike bread always served

English Christmas dinner

With turkey serve stuffing, sweet and mashed → potatoes, broccoli, cranberries, and Regal Plum Pudding (see *Plum Pudding* for recipe).

with a joint of beef roast) and Lancashire hot pot (England's version of Irish stew) have retained regional names but are popular throughout the island.

Northern Englishmen rely on heavy foods to sustain them through colder weather much like their Norman ancestors and Scottish neighbors. Hearty main dishes include the thin stew lobscouse (or scouse for short) and hot pots (stews baked in casseroles). Large round scones called singing hinnys and cakelike breads known as fat rascals are griddle-baked in Scottish fashion. Spicy gingerbread is a common and very popular northern dessert.

Middle England, known as the midlands, is the home of world-famous Cheshire and Stilton cheeses as well as some unique desserts. Cheshire cheese's characteristic saltiness is due to the cows feeding on the grasses of Cheshire county's extremely salty soil. Because of this, Cheshire cheese cannot be reproduced in any other part of the world. Stilton, first made around Stilton, England, is a mellow, blue-veined cheese based on very rich milk. A tour of the countryside also uncovers cream-filled brandy snaps, Mothering Sunday and Easter simnel cake (a spicy cake topped with 12 marzipan balls), and Banbury tarts (pastries filled with spiced dried fruit).

Because the early Celtic tribes were little troubled by foreigners, the southwest region of England, which includes Cornwall, Devon, Somerset, and Dorset counties, contains some of the most unique cooking traditions. A myriad of fish and seafood dishes as well as dairy products are used. Specialties such as Cornish pasties (meal-in-one meat pies), Devonshire cream, Cheddar cheese, rich and sweet Sally Lunn cakes, and caraway-flavored Bath buns had their beginnings with these people.

London and the surrounding area of southeastern England includes a conglomerate of the cuisine styles found throughout the island. Some of its own contributions include fruit tarts and teacakes such as Richmond's maids of honor.

As can be seen, English cookery embraces many kinds of delicious foods. Although many are closely allied to traditional feasts and reserved for special occasions, others are used in everyday meals.

Stuffed Cornish Game Hens

Cook 1½ cups long-grain rice according to package directions. Add ⅓ cup dry red wine, 1½ teaspoons sugar, ¾ teaspoon salt, ⅛ teaspoon pepper, ⅛ teaspoon ground nutmeg, and ⅛ teaspoon ground allspice; mix well. Add ⅓ cup toasted, slivered almonds; stuff lightly into cavities of 6 Cornish game hens, 1 to 1½ pounds each. Place hens in shallow roasting pan; cover loosely with foil.

Roast at 400° for 30 minutes. Uncover and bake 1 hour more, basting occasionally with *Wine Glaze:* Combine ¼ cup dry red wine, 3 tablespoons melted butter or margarine, and 1½ teaspoons lemon juice. Makes 6 servings.

Beef and Kidney Pie

In saucepan combine 1 beef kidney, 1 quart lukewarm water, and 1 teaspoon salt. Soak 1 hour; drain. Cover kidney with cold water. Bring to boiling; simmer 20 minutes. Drain; remove kidney membrane and hard parts, if any. Cut meat in ½-inch cubes; set aside.

Coat 1 pound round steak, cut in ½-inch cubes, with ¼ cup all-purpose flour. In Dutch oven brown beef steak cubes in 3 tablespoons hot shortening. Add 1 medium onion, sliced, 2 cups water, and 1 teaspoon Worcestershire sauce. Cover; simmer till tender, 30 minutes.

In shaker mixer combine ½ cup cold water, ¼ cup all-purpose flour, 1 teaspoon salt, and dash pepper. Stir mixture into hot steak mixture. Cook and stir till mixture is thickened and bubbly. Add cooked kidney cubes; heat through. Pour meat mixture into 1½-quart casserole. Cover with Pastry Topping. Turn under edge and flute. Cut slits for escape of steam. Brush top of pastry with milk. Bake at 450° till golden, 20 to 25 minutes.

Pastry Topping: Sift together 1½ cups all-purpose flour and ½ teaspoon salt; cut in ½ cup shortening with pastry blender till pieces are the size of small peas. Sprinkle 1 tablespoon cold water over part of mixture. Gently toss with fork; push to side of bowl. Repeat with 3 to 4 tablespoons more water till all is moistened. Form into a ball.

Flatten on lightly floured surface by pressing with edge of hand 3 times across in both directions. Roll the dough in circle ½ to 1 inch larger than the casserole dish.

Crispy English Muffins are baked to a delicate brownness on
a top-of-the-range griddle. The cooled muffins are split and
toasted, then spread with lots of butter and marmalade.

ENGLISH MUFFIN—A small, round yeast bread baked on a griddle. The baked muffins are usually split and toasted, then spread with butter and jam or marmalade. They can also be used under creamed foods in casseroles or other such dishes.

These muffins were once sold by street vendors in England; hence, they are called English muffins. (See also *Bread*.)

English Muffins

Spread liberally with butter and jam—

    1 package active dry yeast
5¾ to 6 cups sifted all-purpose flour
    2 cups milk
    ¼ cup shortening
    2 tablespoons sugar
    2 teaspoons salt

In large mixer bowl combine yeast and 2¼ *cups* flour. Heat milk, shortening, sugar, and salt just till warm, stirring occasionally to melt shortening. Add to dry mixture in mixing bowl. Beat at low speed with electric mixer for ½ minute, scraping sides of bowl constantly. Beat 3 minutes at high speed. By hand, stir in enough of the remaining flour to make a moderately stiff dough. Turn out on lightly floured surface; knead till smooth (8 to 10 minutes). Place in greased bowl, turning once. Cover; let rise till double (1¼ hours).

Punch down; cover and let rest 10 minutes. Roll dough to slightly less than ½ inch on lightly floured surface. Cut with a 3-inch round cutter. (Reroll edges.) Cover; let rise till very light (1¼ hours). Bake on top of range on medium-hot greased griddle; turn muffins frequently till done, about 30 minutes. Cool thoroughly. Split muffins with a fork; toast both sides. Serve at once. Makes 24 muffins.

ENGLISH MUSTARD—A powder made from ground mustard seeds. Before using, this powder is mixed with water, vinegar, or flat beer. The resulting mustard sauce is very hot. (See also *Mustard*.)

EN PAPILLOTE *(än pa pē yôt')*—The French word for food enclosed in a paper bag and baked. This method aids in retaining the food's shape and juiciness.

ENRICHED—Flour, cereal, or bakery products to which small amounts of vitamins and/or minerals have been added to improve their nutritive quality. The addition of these vitamins and minerals does not change the food's appearance or flavor.

In the late 1930s, nutritionists became concerned about the deficiency of certain vitamins and minerals in the average American's diet. This concern led to the enrichment, beginning in 1941, of several cereal foods including white bread, all-purpose flour, macaroni products, farina, white rice, and cornmeal. Although this enrichment is not mandatory, over half the states have adopted enrichment laws.

Today, almost all the all-purpose flour sold on the retail market is enriched. In the United States, enriched foods contribute a significant part of the thiamine, riboflavin, niacin, and iron consumed.

ENTRECOTE *(än truh kōt')*—A French word meaning "between the ribs." On a menu, an entrecote beef cut indicates a boneless steak similar to a sirloin steak.

ENTRÉE *(an' trā)*—A French word meaning "entrance." Originally entrée referred to the first course of a meal or the course served between the soup and roast. In the United States, however, it now refers to the main course of a meal.

ENTREMET *(än truh mā')*—A dish served in addition to the main course. In France, an entremet is the sweet course (other than cake or pastry), served after the cheese.

ENZYME *(en' zīm)*—A protein substance produced by living cells in plants and animals that causes chemical changes without being changed itself.

The enzymes in foods are responsible for both desirable and undesirable changes. Enzyme action is important in the ripening of fruits and vegetables. However, once the food has reached maturity, continuing enzyme action results in spoilage characterized by browning, soft spots, and off-flavors. The darkening of cut, fresh fruits such as apples and bananas is caused by enzymes. One of the enzymes in uncooked pineapple breaks down gelatin protein so the gelatin won't set. Therefore, fresh or frozen pineapple must be cooked before it is used in gelatin dishes.

The knowledge that enzymes are inactivated by acids, foods, or heat is applied in several cooking techniques. Apple, banana, pear, and peach pieces will not darken as fast if dipped in lemon juice. The heating of canned foods inactivates enzymes to prevent spoilage from enzyme action. Although freezing foods will slow down enzyme action, it does not inactivate the enzymes. Vegetables, for example, are blanched (heated for a short period of time) before being frozen.

EQUIPMENT—Apparatus used in performing an activity such as food preparation.

Ever since man learned to cook his food over the campfire, he has been using cooking equipment. The remnants of utensils found by archeologists have been extremely important in piecing together the story of man. The first cooking utensil was probably a green stick used to hold food over the fire. Shells were also used by early man as a spoonlike tool. As man became more advanced, he covered woven baskets with clay mud and when they had dried, he used them as water vessels.

After the discovery of metal, man began using metal cooking utensils and tools. Later a reflector-type oven was made for baking bread. In ancient Egypt, an enclosed oven was made. Glass, which was made by fusing sand and soda ash, was another cooking utensil of ancient Egypt.

Through the centuries, man has perfected these ancient materials and equipment designs and has discovered so many new things that today we have an abundant choice of cooking equipment in a variety of materials, colors, sizes, and styles.

Basic kitchen needs: In cooking, the production of the finished dish depends not only on the proper handling of food materials but also on the use of proper equipment and utensils. The equipment needed for food preparation can be broken down into five groups—storage, preparation, cooking, cleaning, and serving. In each of these groups, there are numerous articles available. The box at right, however, is limited to the equipment needed to initially supply a kitchen. As money and need arise, other convenient but less essential equipment can be added.

How to select: Food preparation is one of the homemaker's basic duties, so it is important to select kitchen equipment carefully. Since this group includes a broad range of items, it is difficult to give specific selection guides. The following points, however, should be considered when purchasing any kitchen equipment.

1. Materials and structure. Is this piece of equipment sturdy and durable? Is the material easy to clean and suitable for this piece of equipment? (Metal handles might get hot and plastic measuring cups may bend and not give accurate measurements.) Will the material stain or rust? Will the finish peel off? Are all the handles securely fastened? Are all the electrical terminals safely recessed?

2. Design. Are there any hard-to-clean cracks or crevices? Does the design coordinate with the other kitchen equipment? Are there any sharp edges?

3. Storage. Is there space to store this where it will be readily available?

4. Use. What can this be used for? Does another model offer features that will increase the possibilities of use?

5. Price. Will another model or another store give more for the money?

6. Seals of approval, standards, and testing. Gas appliances should have American Gas Assocation seal. Look for the Underwriters' Laboratory seal on electrical appliances. Measuring utensils should have "U.S. Standard Measures" on the package to show they have been standardized.

7. Manufacturer and dealer. Will they stand behind the product? Do they provide servicing? Are they well known?

Basic kitchen equipment

Storage

refrigerator/freezer	cupboards
assorted refrigerator- freezer dishes	bread box
	canisters
foil; clear plastic wrap	waxed paper

Preparation

can opener	utility slicer
grater or shredder	carving knife
vegetable peeler	potato masher
kitchen shears	vegetable brush
pair of tongs	strainers
2 paring knives	colander
serrated knife	electric mixer
nested set of dry measuring cups	wooden spoons
	flour sifter
measuring spoons	rotary beater
set of mixing bowls	bottle opener
liquid measuring cup	rubber spatula
rolling pin with cover	pastry cloth

Cooking

covered skillets (10- and 7-to 8-inch)	range with oven
	tube pan
covered saucepans (1, 2, and 4 to 6 quarts)	square pans
	coffee maker
wire cooling rack	pancake turner
long-handled fork	toaster
long-handled spoon	jelly roll pan
oblong pan (13x9x2)	round cake pans
loaf dish (8½x4½x2½)	muffin pan
roasting pan, rack	custard cups
casserole with cover	cookie sheets
pot holders; hot pads	pie plates

Cleaning

sink	dishpan
dishcloth and towels	wastebasket
draining rack, mat	garbage pail

Serving

serving bowls	platter
dinner and salad plates	sauce dishes
cups and saucers	glasses
table linen	silverware

ESCALLOPE, ESCALLOPED—To bake foods, topped with crumbs, in a cream sauce in a casserole or individual baking dish. At one time the term was used to refer to foods that were served in scallop shells, hence the term escalloped. (See also *Scalloped.*)

ESCARGOT (*e skar gō'*)—The French word for an edible, land snail. Escargot is often used on restaurant menus for snails or dishes made of snails. (See also *Snail.*)

ESCAROLE (*es' kuh rōl'*)—Broad-leafed variety of endive most often used for salads. Native to the East Indies and known to have been grown in ancient Greece and Egypt, escarole was introduced to the United States by early colonists.

Escarole is often considered a winter salad green but is available all year around. When selecting a head of escarole in the market, look for tender, crisp, fresh, green leaves enclosing a heart of blanched creamy white or yellow white leaves. The leaves should snap easily between the fingers. Toughness and excessive bitterness of this endive variety are indicated by wilted and brownish outer leaves.

The flattened escarole bunches, with broad, slightly curled leaves, have a firm texture. The green leaves shade into yellows close to the center of the head. Because escarole has a slightly bitter flavor, it is usually combined with other greens and fresh vegetables for salads.

A head of escarole should be thoroughly washed before using to remove any sand. If any sand remains, soak the head for a short time. Then cut off and discard the bitter roots. The clean salad green is then torn into pieces instead of being cut with a knife. Escarole should be chilled in the refrigerator, as any salad green, well before serving time.

As a salad ingredient, escarole can be tossed with oil and vinegar, or mixed with other salad greens and served with any favorite salad dressing. You can also use it as a boiled and lightly salted table vegetable with cheese and cream sauces poured over it. Or, use it as part of a delectable soup. Preparation methods and recipes for endive and chicory can also be used for escarole. (See also *Endive.*)

Slightly bitter escarole has green outer leaves shading to yellow closer to center. Well-branched heart appears bleached.

ESCHALOT (*esh' uh lot', esh' uh lot'*)—The French word for shallot, a member of the onion family. The gray or brownish bulbs are divided into cloves similar to garlic. This mild, delicate-flavored herb is used in meat dishes, fish, poultry, and sauces, or when combined with onions, is often used in salads and soups.

ESPAGNOLE SAUCE (*es' puhn yōl', -pan-*)—A basic brown sauce from which other sauces can be made. Espagnole sauce is made with a rich stock of brown roux or bouillon and simmered several hours. It becomes quite thick after it has boiled down. French cooks take espagnole sauce a step further and make it into a demi-glace. The sauce may contain tomatoes or tomato paste, fruit juices, or vegetable stocks. It may be flavored with sherry wine, if desired. (See also *Sauce.*)

ESPRESSO COFFEE (*e spres' o*)—A dark, strong coffee made in a special coffee machine by forcing hot water or steam pressure through finely ground roasted coffee. To make espresso coffee in the home, purchase an imported machine from a specialty shop, or use a three part coffee maker similar to a drip-type coffeemaker. Instant espresso coffee is also available in some shops or supermarkets for those people not wanting to invest in the special equipment required to brew espresso coffee.

Originally Italian, the after-dinner espresso coffee is usually served in small demitasse cups; for an added delight, garnish it with a lemon twist or serve it with tiny dollops of whipped cream on top of the coffee. (See also *Coffee.*)

ESSENCE—Concentrated, oily liquid or extract possessing the smell, taste, nutritive value, or color of some plant or food. The commercial preparation is obtained by distillation or infusion.

Jellylike meat essences, such as beef essence, are made from concentrated meat juices and are used to enhance the flavor of dishes such as soups, sauces, stews, and gravies. The rich, essential oils in alcoholic solutions are usually volatile.

Essences resemble extracts in that they are flavor additions in concentrated form.

EST EST EST—A golden, semisweet wine made from the Moscatello grapes of Montefiascone in the Lazio region (north of Rome), Italy. There are two different types of the Italian wine that vary in sweetness, with the sweetest one most often preferred.

The name "Est! Est! Est!" (It is! It is! It is!) was given to this renowned beverage in honor of a wine-loving German bishop, who used to take long journeys and would send a trusty servant ahead to check the lodging and to taste the wines.

Whenever the servant came across an acceptable lodge offering good wines he was to write "Est!" on the wall. Upon tasting the superb wine of Montefiascone, the servant wrote "Est! Est! Est!" on the wall. The bishop agreed with his enthusiasm after arriving and proceeded to drink himself to death. (See also *Wine and Spirits.*)

ESTOUFFADE (*es' too fad'*)—1. A rich meat stew cooked very slowly in a covered casserole dish with seasonings and a small amount of liquid. 2. A light brown stock made of meats, vegetables, and seasonings used to dilute sauces for meats and casseroles and used in jellies and stews.

ESTRAGON (*es' truh gon'*)—The French name for the herb terragon. The mysterious sweet, bitter taste resembling anise makes estragon an excellent companion to vinegars and sauces, and fish or chicken dishes. Mix the fragrant estragon leaves with butter and serve with cold dishes.

ÉTOUFFÉ (*e tu' fe*)—A French cooking method in which foods are simmered, sometimes covered, in very little liquid. The liquid may be water, stock, or wine. The foods, either meats, poultry, or vegetables, are smothered in their own juices.

Shrimp Étouffé

    1 medium onion, finely chopped
    2 green onions, finely chopped
    3 or 4 cloves garlic, minced
 1/4 cup chopped celery
 1/2 cup butter or margarine
    2 tablespoons all-purpose flour
    1 10½-ounce can tomato purée
    2 bay leaves
    1 tablespoon Worcestershire sauce
    4 drops bottled hot pepper sauce
    1 teaspoon salt
 1/2 teaspoon sugar
 1/2 teaspoon dried thyme leaves,
       crushed
 1/8 teaspoon pepper
    3 cups cleaned raw shrimp
       (about 1½ pounds)

Cook onion, green onions, garlic, and celery in butter till tender. Add flour; cook and stir till lightly browned. Add all remaining ingredients except shrimp. Stir in 2½ cups water.

Simmer, uncovered, stirring occasionally, till almost of desired consistency, about 25 minutes. Add shrimp; cook 15 minutes more. If desired, garnish with wedges of hard-cooked egg.

EVAPORATED MILK—Milk from which about 60 percent of the water has been removed during processing for canning. The two types are evaporated milk, made from whole fresh milk, and evaporated skimmed milk, made from skimmed milk. The concentrated canned milk is lower priced than the same amount of fresh milk in terms of milk solids. No sugar is added to the evaporated milk which must conform to federal standards. The sterilized milk is easy to store and efficiently transported without refrigeration.

How evaporated milk is produced: Evaporated milk is made by heating whole milk in a vacuum evaporator. About 60 percent of the water is removed in the process and the milk is homogenized, then cooled and put in 6- or 14½-ounce cans or 6¾-pound institutional cans.

The sealed cans are then sterilized for ten to fifteen minutes at 245° to 250° F. This sterilization prevents any bacterial spoilage and makes storage without refrigeration possible. A stabilizer is often added to the evaporated milk.

Nutritional value: According to federal regulation, evaporated milk must contain not less than 7.9 percent milk fat and not less than 25.9 percent total milk solids. All brands of evaporated milk have vitamin D added to fortify nutrition.

How to store: Store unopened cans of evaporated milk on the kitchen shelf. Store opened cans of evaporated milk in the refrigerator and use within a few days as you would any fresh milk product.

How to use: Add equal amounts of water to evaporated milk to use as whole, fresh milk. For some recipes, it is interesting to reconstitute the milk with vegetable liquids, fruit juices, or broths.

For a smooth texture, use evaporated milk in creamed and scalloped dishes, custards, sauces, and candies. It is also excellent when used for binding, coating, and emulsifying purposes. (See also *Milk*.)

How to whip evaporated milk

Freeze milk in freezer trays till soft ice crystals form around the edges. Whip the evaporated milk until stiff peaks form and the mixture triples in volume. Sweeten whipped evaporated milk with sugar to taste.

Tomato Aspic Soufflé

Pour one 6-ounce can evaporated milk into freezer tray. Freeze milk till soft ice crystals form around edges. In medium saucepan blend 2 cups tomato juice with 2 bay leaves; 4 black peppercorns; ½ teaspoon onion salt; ¼ teaspoon celery salt; and ¼ teaspoon dried oregano leaves, crushed. Simmer mixture, covered, for 5 minutes; strain with sieve.

Soften 2 envelopes (2 tablespoons) unflavored gelatin in an additional ½ cup cold tomato juice; stir into hot mixture till gelatin is dissolved. Cool thoroughly. With rotary beater, gradually beat an additional ½ cup tomato juice into two 3-ounce packages softened cream cheese; stir into gelatin mixture.

Chill mixture till partially set. Whip icy cold evaporated milk till stiff peaks form; fold whipped milk into gelatin mixture. Pour mixture into 6½-cup mold; chill till firm. Unmold at serving time. Makes 10 to 12 servings.

Chicken Loaf

      4 cups coarsely ground, cooked
         chicken (1 4- to 5-pound
         stewing chicken)
   1½ cups soft bread crumbs
         (about 2½ slices bread)
      1 6-ounce can evaporated milk
      2 slightly beaten eggs
    ⅓ cup chicken broth
    ⅔ cup finely chopped celery
    ¼ cup chopped canned pimiento
    ¾ teaspoon salt
         Dash pepper
         Dash dried rosemary leaves,
            crushed
         Dash dried marjoram leaves,
            crushed
         Dash ground nutmeg
         Mushroom Sauce

Lightly combine all ingredients except Mushroom Sauce. Line bottom of greased 8½x4½x2½-inch loaf dish with foil; grease foil. Turn mixture into dish. Bake at 350° till center is firm about 45 minutes. Invert on platter; remove foil. Serve with Mushroom Sauce.

Mushroom Sauce: Combine one 10½-ounce can condensed cream of mushroom soup with ⅓ cup milk; heat thoroughly. Makes 6 servings.

Pumpkin-Orange Crunch Pie

    1 cup brown sugar
    1 tablespoon cornstarch
1½ teaspoons pumpkin pie spice
    1 16-ounce can pumpkin (2 cups)
    1 14½-ounce can evaporated
       milk (1⅔ cups)
    2 slightly beaten eggs
    1 *unbaked* 9-inch pastry shell
       (See *Pastry*)
    1 tablespoon brown sugar
    1 tablespoon butter or margarine
    1 tablespoon all-purpose flour
  ½ cup chopped walnuts
    2 teaspoons grated orange peel

Combine 1 cup brown sugar, cornstarch, pie spice, ¼ teaspoon salt, and pumpkin. Stir in milk and eggs. Pour into pastry shell. (Crimp edges high—filling is generous.) Bake at 400° for 40 minutes. Meanwhile, combine remaining ingredients. Spoon mixture over pie; return to oven and bake till knife comes out clean, about 5 to 10 minutes more. Cool.

Apple-Walnut Cobbler

  ½ cup sugar
  ½ teaspoon ground cinnamon
  ¾ cup coarsely chopped walnuts
    4 cups thinly sliced, peeled
       tart apples
       · · ·
    1 cup sifted all-purpose flour
    1 cup sugar
    1 teaspoon baking powder
  ¼ teaspoon salt
    1 well-beaten egg
  ½ cup evaporated milk
  ⅓ cup butter or margarine, melted

Mix ½ cup sugar, the cinnamon, and ½ *cup walnuts*. Place apples in bottom of a greased 8¼x1¾-inch round ovenware cake dish. Sprinkle with the cinnamon mixture. Sift together dry ingredients. Combine egg, milk, and butter; add dry ingredients all at once and mix till smooth. Pour over apples; sprinkle with remaining walnuts. Bake at 325° till done, about 55 minutes. Spoon warm cobbler onto dessert plates. If desired, top with cinnamon whipped cream or ice cream. Makes 8 servings.

Honey-Banana Mold

Pour one 6-ounce can evaporated milk into freezer tray. Freeze milk till soft ice crystals form around edges of freezer tray.

Dissolve one 3-ounce package orange-flavored gelatin in 1 cup boiling water; cool mixture. Peel 2 ripe medium bananas; mash in large mixer bowl with electric mixer. Beat in ¼ cup honey and 3 tablespoons lemon juice, then cooled gelatin. Chill till mixture is partially set.

Whip mixture at low speed with electric mixer while gradually adding icy cold milk. Increase to high speed; continue whipping till mixture is double in volume and thick. Pour into 4½-cup mold. Chill till firm. Serves 4 to 6.

Asparagus with Two-Cheese Sauce

Wash and cook fresh asparagus spears, covered, in small amount boiling, salted water for 10 to 15 minutes; drain thoroughly.

Beat one 8-ounce package softened cream cheese till smooth; gradually beat in ½ cup evaporated milk. Cook and stir over medium heat till hot. Stir in dash salt and 1 tablespoon grated Parmesan cheese. Pour over hot cooked asparagus spears; sprinkle with an additional 1 tablespoon Parmesan cheese. Makes ¾ cup.

EXTRACT—Concentrated flavorings secured by boiling or distillation. The condensed flavors are extracted from meats, vegetables, liquids, or seasonings. The degree of evaporation is controlled to produce a liquid extract, such as vanilla, or a solid extract, such as a bouillon cube.

The liquid extracts of vanilla, mint, lemon, peppermint, almond, and others are dissolved in an alcohol solution and are volatile. Of the two liquid types, pure and imitation extracts, imitation has fuller flavor. Both liquid and solid extracts are used as flavoring additions.

EXTRA DRY—Term used to indicate the opposite of sweet when speaking of wines and spirits. The grape sugar is fermented into alcohol resulting in a light flavor good for most food accompaniments. Champagne is an example of an extra dry wine. (See also *Wine and Spirits*.)

F

FAGOT (*fag' et*) — 1. A *bouquet garni* made by tying seasonings and vegetables with a string. 2. A pork liver pattie that is most often baked in the oven.

Season soups and stews as well as braised meats or vegetables with a fagot used as a bouquet garni. The bundle, tied securely with a string, most often includes celery, bay leaf, parsley, thyme, and other herbs specified by the recipe or personal taste. Before serving, the fagot is easily removed from the stew or meat.

Fagot pork patties made of pork liver, crumbs, seasonings, and pork fat are sold in some meat departments ready to bake.

FANTAN ROLL — Dainty rolls made by stacking long strips of dough and cutting through strips for each roll. The rolls are placed with cut side down in muffin pan and allowed to bake.

For variation, fantan rolls are brushed with melted butter and sprinkled with sesame or poppy seed before baking. The tops of the rolls fan out slightly as they bake and become lightly browned.

Use convenient ready-to-bake butterflake rolls for quick and easy preparation of the classic fantan rolls. Make them for special occasions by separating the sections slightly and brushing with an herb-flavored butter which would be compatible with the particular meal. (See also *Roll*.)

Fantans

Divide Basic Roll Dough (see *Roll*) in 3 equal pieces and round each in a ball. Cover; let rest 10 minutes. Roll each ball in a 14x9-inch rectangle, about ¼ inch thick. Brush with melted butter or margarine.

Cut each rectangle lengthwise in 6 strips, 1½ inches wide (see picture). Pile all 6 strips on top of one another; cut in 1½-inch lengths, making 9 pieces (see picture). Place cut side down in greased muffin pans. Cover rolls and let rise in warm place till double in size, about 1 to 1½ hours. Bake at 375° till done, about 15 minutes. Makes 27 rolls.

Parsley Fantans

> 2 tablespoons butter
> 1 teaspoon lemon juice
> 2 tablespoons snipped parsley
> 2 tablespoons snipped chives
> 6 brown-and-serve butterflake
>   rolls

Melt butter; add lemon juice. Combine parsley and chives. Partially separate sections of brown-and-serve rolls. Brush sections with some butter; sprinkle with part of parsley-chive mixture. Place in muffin cups. Brush with remaining butter; sprinkle with parsley and chives. Brown at 400° for 10 minutes.

Cut Fantans from 14x9-inch rectangle of Basic Roll Dough. Slit each rectangle lengthwise in six strips 1½-inches wide.

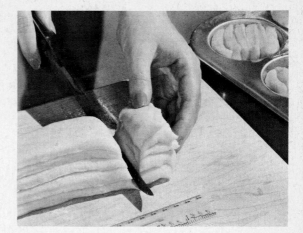

Stack six strips on top of another and cut in nine 1½-inch lengths. Place Fantans cut side down in greased muffin pan.

FARCE—A French word meaning stuffing or forcemeat, generally ground meat, used as a filling. Farce is made from finely ground meats, poultry, or fish combined with a wide variety of seasonings and vegetables. Combinations include pork and herb, rice and kidney, and ham and mushroom.

Fix-up Parsley Fantans in a hurry with ready-to-bake butterflake rolls. Serve with a salad for a light lunch.

FARCI—1. French word meaning stuffed or filled. 2. Any one of a number of stuffed French food dishes. Various food dishes which originated in the southern part of France are referred to as farci. The most commonly served farci dish is stuffed cabbage leaves cooked in stock.

FARFEL—Pastalike mixture of flour, eggs, and water cooked in boiling water to use as an accompaniment or in dumplings. The egg mixture is formed into noodles which become quite crumbly. A speciality of Jewish cookery, farfel is often used as a substitute for potatoes and can be served with goulash to complete a meal.

FARINA—The granular, center portion of hard wheat kernel from which bran and germ have been removed. The finely ground cereal is sometimes combined with protein splitting enzymes and a salt to cause the particles to swell faster and cook more quickly. This is why it is important to check the label when cooking farina.

Farina is most often enriched with iron and the various B vitamins. This makes farina valuable as a breakfast cereal and baby food. Because of its bland flavor, farina combines well with other foods to make puddings, muffins, baked desserts, and dumplings. (See also *Wheat*.)

FARMER CHEESE—A pressed-curd cheese related to cottage cheese. Also known as farm cheese and pressed cheese, farmer cheese was originally made in France. Processing methods differ according to locality, so all farmer cheese is not the same. The tangy-flavored farmer cheese made in the United States cuts smooth without crumbling. (See also *Cottage Cheese.*)

FASTNACHTKUCHEN (*fash' näkt kōōk uhn, fäs-, -kûh-*)—The Pennsylvania-Dutch name for rectangular or round doughnuts. Traditionally served the night before fasting began for Lent, the word means fast-night cake. (See *Doughnut, Pennsylvania-Dutch Cookery* for additional information.)

FAT—A class of foods from animal and vegetable sources; in solid form called fat and in liquid form called oil. Fats are a source of essential fatty acids, carry fat-soluble vitamins, and contribute energy in concentrated form. Every cook knows the value of fats for adding flavor and aroma to many foods, as a shortening in baked foods, and as a preservative.

Nutritional value: Besides supplying essential fatty acids and making fat-soluble vitamins available to the body, fats provide more energy per gram than any other food source. In fact, nutritionists figure nine calories per gram for fats to four calories per gram for proteins or carbohydrates. Fats are stored in the body and converted to energy as needed; thus protein is not needed for energy and can be used for body-building purposes instead. Also, although easily digested, fats are absorbed slowly and delay the return of the sensation of hunger.

Fats are eaten as spreads on bread or as an ingredient in other foods. One tablespoon of butter or margarine contains 100 calories. Of course, calories are contributed to any food to which fat is added.

Currently, there is much discussion and research on the relationship of dietary fats and cholesterol. The terms saturated, unsaturated, and polyunsaturated refer to how the hydrogen atoms in a fat molecule are linked together. Saturated fats contain single-bond linkages; unsaturated fats have one double-bond linkage; and polyunsaturated fats contain more than one double-bond linkage.

Types and kinds: Fats that are solid at room temperature include butter, margarine, hydrogenated shortening, and lard. Fats that are liquid at room temperature are usually referred to as oils.

By law, butter must contain 80 percent natural milk fat. Margarine, similar to butter in flavor, color and cooking uses, can be made with animal or vegetable fat combined with milk or cream.

Today, shortenings used in the home and commercially include vegetable shortenings, vegetable and animal fat combinations, and lards that are processed from pork fat. The shortening grandmother used most often was lard rendered from animal fats and was quite different from the soft, white lards that supermarkets now stock.

Salad oils and cooking oils are made principally from cottonseed, corn, and soybean oils, although olive, peanut, and safflower oils are also used. Vegetable oils are refined to produce a bland, odorless product without added moisture.

Although many of these fats are used interchangeably, butter and margarine are used primarily as spreads, lard, and vegetable shortening are used most often for baking and frying, and the oils are basic ingredients in homemade and commercial salad dressings and mayonnaise.

How products from fats and oils are processed: With the exception of butter which is churned from cream, the processing of fats and oils, regardless of ultimate use, begins with three steps that remove undesirable elements: refining removes impurities; bleaching removes color-producing substances; deodorization eliminates undesirable aromas and flavors. When manufacturers wish to turn a liquid oil into a semisolid shortening with improved stability and excellent creaming properties, they expose the oil to hydrogen in a process called hydrogenation.

Cooking value: Fats and oils probably have a wider range of table and cooking uses than any other kind of food. The most obvious example of their versatility is the use of butter and margarine as flavor enhancers for spreading on bread, and for seasoning cooked vegetables.

Another popular use of fats and oils is for frying. When properly prepared, fried foods are wholesome and easily digested. Select the type of fat according to the temperature to be used for frying. Butter and margarine, for instance, smoke at a fairly low temperature, called the smoke point, and thus are suitable only for sautéeing and quick, light frying.

For high-temperature and deep-fat frying, vegetable oils (except olive), all-purpose shortenings (hydrogenated or not), and some high-quality lards are best because they have high smoke points.

The word shortening describes the action of the fat in baking and explains how fats create tenderness in pastries and other baked goods: the fat, surrounding the flour particles, breaks up or "shortens" the gluten strands that form the framework of the cake or bread; hence a more tender product. When creamed for baked products, the shortening traps air in the batter for leavening. In pastry the shortening melts during baking leaving air spaces which produce the desired flakiness. As the shortening melts, it also dissolves and blends the seasonings. Shortenings include butter, margarine, lard, hydrogenated shortening, and a very large variety of vegetable oils.

The emulsifying properties of oils determine the textures of salad dressings. Commercial salad dressings and mayonnaise must contain a certain percentage of fat and oil as specified by law.

As a preservative, fats and oils prevent exposure of foods to air which can cause drying and decomposition. That is why canned fish is often packed in oil. Since oils do not blend readily with other liquids, a thin layer will keep the air from reaching the liquid's surface. Try it on an unfinished bottle of wine. Just put a drop of oil on the surface of the wine to preserve its flavor and good quality.

How to select: Table spreads are marketed by the pound or quarter pound, in tubs, and in whipped form. Oils are available in bottles or cans, in liquid or ounce measures. Lards and vegetable shortenings are packed in one- to three-pound containers. Purchase the right size and kind of fat by considering your family's needs, tastes, and size. Another important point to consider is the size of your refrigerator; fats require careful storage.

How to store: Exposure to air, heat, light, or moisture causes a chemical change in most fats and oils; a decomposition and unpalatable taste and aroma called "rancidity." Some fats and oils are specially processed to contain antioxidants that retard rancidity. Because oxygen in the air causes rancidity, and heat speeds the damage, proper storage of fats and oils at home is important. Butter and margarine absorb odors quickly and should be kept tightly covered in the refrigerator. Salad oils should be stored in a cool place. Some lards need to be refrigerated, others may be kept on the kitchen shelf if the room is relatively cool. Keep all lards covered and check the labels for storage directions. All-purpose shortenings have been stabilized during processing and need only be kept in a closed container at room temperature to maintain and prolong their nutritional value. (See *Nutrition,* individual fats and oils for additional information.)

How to measure fats and oils

Correct measuring methods using standard measuring equipment are important to the quality of the recipe being prepared.

Solid fats
Press firmly in a measuring spoon or individual measuring cup, making sure all air bubbles are pressed out.

Cut with a knife at tablespoon equivalents marked on moisture-proof wrappers of quarter pound butter or margarine.

Oils and melted fats
Measure, as you do any liquid, in a measuring spoon or liquid measuring cup.

FATTIGMANN—A Norwegian deep-fat fried Christmas cookie. The name means poor man, and the cookie may be served either plain or with a jam or jelly. (See also *Scandinavian Cookery*.)

Fattigmann

        6 egg yolks
      ¼ cup sugar
        1 tablespoon butter or margarine, melted
      ⅓ cup whipping cream
        2 cups sifted all-purpose flour
        1 teaspoon ground cardamom
      ½ teaspoon salt

Beat egg yolks till thick and lemon-colored; gradually beat in sugar. Gently stir in butter or margarine. Whip cream till soft peaks form. Fold into egg mixture. Sift together flour, cardamom, and salt; gradually fold just enough flour into yolk mixture to make a soft dough. Chill dough thoroughly.

Divide dough in half. On lightly floured surface, roll each half to an ⅛-inch thickness. Cut dough in 2-inch wide strips, then slash diagonally at 3-inch lengths to make diamonds. Cut slit in center of each diamond and pull one end through. Fry a few at time in deep hot fat (375°) for 1 to 1½ minutes, till very light golden brown. Drain on paper toweling. While warm, sift a little confectioners' sugar over cookies, if desired. Makes about 5 dozen.

Shape Scandinavian Fattigmanns by pulling one end of the diamond-shaped piece through slash cut in center. Deep-fat fry.

FAVA (*fä′ vuh*)—The Italian name for big, broad beans similar to lima beans. The heavy beans, growing up to eighteen inches long, are often removed from the pod (purchased in pod) before cooking. The beans may also be peeled before cooking. If the beans are young and fresh, the complete bean and pod is eaten.

Known also as the broad bean in Italy, fava beans are boiled till tender in salted water. Sometimes they are then mashed with butter or other oil till of mashed potato consistency. The beans can also be puréed and dressed with cream or cheese and served with pork, chicken, or a variety of other meats. (See also *Bean*.)

FELL—A thin, paperlike membrane covering the outside fat of lamb cuts, such as leg of lamb or lamb chops. The homemaker often removes the fell from most lamb cuts before cooking, except for the larger cuts such as leg of lamb. If the leg of lamb is to be marinated or brushed with a sauce during cooking, the fell should be removed so the flavoring substance can penetrate the meat more thoroughly.

Some homemakers prefer to leave the fell on the leg of lamb cut during cooking. The larger cut of meat will hold its shape better if the fell is left intact. Because the juices are held in by the membrane, the lamb cut will cook faster and be juicier. The fell does not affect the taste of the meat. (See also *Lamb*.)

FENNEL (*fen′ uhl*)—An aromatic plant of the parsley family with a celerylike texture and an anise flavor. Native to southern Europe and the Mediterranean, fennel has enjoyed a number of contrasting uses. The plant was long used as a condiment by the ancient Chinese, Indians, and Egyptians. The Italians and Romans cooked fennel roots and stalk as a vegetable. For medicinal purposes, fennel was used to remedy snake bites, strengthen eyesight, and combat diseases.

The herb was a symbol of success to the Greeks, and was used in the Middle Ages to enhance witchcraft ideas and ceremonies. Early colonists staved off hunger by chewing on sugar coated fennel seed during church services.

The hardy perennial grows from a seed in a moderate climate. After the fennel seeds have turned a greenish gray color and are somewhat hard, they are harvested and dried. Argentina, Bulgaria, and India are among the chief exporters of fennel to the United States.

A small, dwarf variety, known as sweet fennel or Florence fennel, has a broad bulbous base and thick leaf stalks. The sweet fennel bulb and stalks are cooked like a vegetable and have a flavor similar to that of celery.

Fennel, surprisingly rich in vitamin A, is available throughout the year whole (seeds) or ground. The sweet-scented herb is appropriately used for breads, confections, fish, pastry, stews, and pickles. The licorice-flavored fennel is popular in Scandinavian and Italian dishes.

The long-needled leaves are often included in fish sauces and pickles. The leaves can also be minced and the bulbous roots sliced to be used in a fresh salad. The seeds yield an oil adaptable for use in cough drops, pickles, perfumed cosmetics, and licorice candies. (See also *Herb.*)

American Pizza

  ¾ **pound ground beef**
  ⅓ **cup chopped celery**
  ⅓ **cup chopped onion**
  3 **tablespoons chopped green pepper**
  1 **small clove garlic, minced**
  ½ **teaspoon dried oregano leaves,**
    crushed
  ¼ **teaspoon fennel seed**

    • • •

  1 **15½-ounce package cheese pizza**
    mix
  2 **ounces sharp process American**
    cheese, shredded (½ cup)

In skillet cook meat with vegetables till meat is browned and vegetables are tender. Drain off excess fat. Stir in seasonings. Prepare pizza dough following package directions. Roll or pat out to fit 12-inch pizza pan. Crimp edges. Spread pizza sauce (from package mix) over dough. Top with meat, American cheese, then grated cheese (from package mix). Bake at 425° for 25 to 30 minutes. Makes 1 12-inch pizza.

FENUGREEK (*fen' yŏŏ grēk'*) — An aromatic herb of the bean family cultivated for its seed. Native to Asia and southeastern Europe, fenugreek was used by the Egyptians as quinine is used for medicinal purposes today in medicines.

The fenugreek plant is important as a spice, food in the form of a vegetable, cattle forage, and is used sometimes as a medicinal ingredient. The annual plant is grown commercially from a seed. Chief export countries include Argentina, Egypt, France, India, and Lebanon. The small seeds, yellow brown in color, have an irregular shape. The aroma of the seed, available either whole or in ground form, is strong but pleasant.

The flavor of fenugreek, similar to burnt sugar, is well known in the kitchen as it is used commercially in imitation maple syrups, maple flavorings, and maple-flavored candies. The spice, which supplements protein nutritive value as well as adding flavor, is also used in chutneys, curry powders, mango pickles, and condiments. (See also *Herb.*)

FETTUCINI (*fet' uh chē' nē*) — An Italian specialty made of flat egg noodles, cheese, butter, and sometimes cream. The noodles are made of the same flour paste as spaghetti. (See also *Italian Cookery.*)

FIDDLEHEAD GREENS — The tightly curved sprouts of a fern plant that are eaten as a vegetable. The name comes from the violinlike appearance of the curving frond (leaf) of the plant. Growing along the edges of streams, the fern is a well-known vegetable in Maine, in northern New England, and in Canada.

When the sprouts have grown to a length of two inches, in early spring, they are picked. Cooked in boiling, salted water, the fiddlehead greens offer a unique flavor and crunchy texture when served as a hot vegetable. The flavor of fiddlehead greens can best be described as a cross between asparagus and mushrooms.

The greens may also be cut and tossed with an assortment of salad greens and then be dressed with vinegar and lemon juice. Canned fiddlehead greens are available in specialty grocery stores.

FIELD SALAD — A salad green, both wild and cultivated, recognized by its spoon-shaped leaves. Field salad contributes a slightly bitter flavor. Field salad varieties are also called corn salad, lamb's lettuce, fat hen, and hog salad. (See also *Vegetable*.)

FIG — The small, sweet edible fruit of the fig tree grown in warm climates. The fig originated in Asia, Africa, and southern Europe and was introduced to America by early Spanish missionaries.

How figs are produced: California is the chief commercial producing state. Some fig trees are self-pollinating and others must be cross-pollinated by a fig wasp. The blossoms are actually inside the fruit, which explains why the tree has no visible blossoms and why there are such a great number of seeds inside the fruit

Fresh figs are marketed immediately upon becoming ripe. Dried figs are allowed to fully ripen on the tree until heavy with sugar. Partially dried when they drop to the ground, the figs are then dried in the sun, graded, and cleaned.

Nutritional value: The soft fruit is an excellent source of natural fruit sugars which contribute quick energy. Dried figs are rich in iron, calcium, and phosphorus.

Types and kinds: From six to eight hundred varieties of figs, varying in size and color, are grown throughout the world.

The original planting of figs by missionaries in California has led to the development of the many varieties now grown in this country. The Calimyrna is grown in California along with the Adriatic, Black Mission, and Kadota. The varieties, differing in color and size, are sold fresh, dried, or preserved.

The figs common in the southeastern states and Texas and grown chiefly for canning and preserving include the Brown Turkey, Celeste, and Magnolia also called New Brunswick. Each variety is recognized by a different skin and pulp color.

How to select: A fresh fig should feel soft to touch and have a bright, clear color representative of the variety. A charac-

Figs vary in color from green to yellow, brown, purple, or black, depending on variety. The sweet fruit is seed-filled.

teristic aroma, produced by fermentation, is obvious if the fig is not fresh. Fresh figs are available June through October. Figs may also be bought dried or preserved.

How to store: Refrigerate and use fresh figs soon after purchased. Store dried figs in a covered container in a cool place. Refrigerate canned figs after opening.

How to prepare: Peel fresh figs and serve with sugar and cream. Dried figs used for stewing require a short soaking and quick-cooking period. Prepare plump dried figs, for cakes and candies, by soaking them in hot water up to 30 minutes.

How to use: Fresh, dried, and canned figs are used in desserts and confections such as cakes, candies, and puddings. Toss plump figs in salads and fruit compotes. Use figs in dumplings, fritters, breads, and marmalades. (See also *Fruit*.)

fig 871

Applesauce-Fig Loaf

6 tablespoons butter or margarine
⅔ cup sugar
1 egg
1 teaspoon vanilla
2 cups sifted all-purpose flour
1 teaspoon baking powder
1 teaspoon baking soda
½ teaspoon ground cinnamon
¼ teaspoon ground nutmeg
1 cup applesauce
1 cup finely snipped dried figs
½ cup chopped pecans

Cream butter or margarine and sugar till fluffy. Add egg and vanilla; blend well. Sift together flour, baking powder, baking soda, cinnamon, and nutmeg; add to creamed mixture alternately with applesauce. Stir in figs and nuts. Pour into greased 9x5x3-inch loaf pan and bake at 350° till done, about 1 hour. Cool in pan about 20 minutes; remove and cool on rack.

Fig-Nut Squares

½ cup butter or margarine
1¾ cups brown sugar
4 well-beaten eggs
1 teaspoon grated lemon peel
1 teaspoon grated orange peel
2 cups snipped dried figs *or* dates
1 cup chopped walnuts
1½ cups sifted all-purpose flour
1 teaspoon baking powder
½ teaspoon salt
• • •
Creamy Hard Sauce

Melt butter; stir in brown sugar. Add eggs; mix well. Stir in lemon and orange peel, *half* the figs, and *half* the nuts. Sift together dry ingredients. Blend into batter. Pour into greased 13x9x2-inch baking pan. Sprinkle batter with remaining figs and nuts. Bake at 325° for approximately 50 to 55 minutes.

Creamy Hard Sauce: Thoroughly cream together ¼ cup butter or margarine and 2 cups sifted confectioners' sugar. Add 3 tablespoons milk and 1 teaspoon vanilla; mix well. Whip ½ cup whipping cream; fold into creamed mixture. Pass with fig squares. Serves 12.

Fig Bars

1 cup shortening
½ cup granulated sugar
½ cup brown sugar
1 egg
¼ cup milk
1 teaspoon vanilla
3 cups sifted all-purpose flour
½ teaspoon salt
½ teaspoon baking soda
• • •
Fig Filling

Cream shortening and sugars. Add egg, milk, and vanilla; beat well. Sift together dry ingredients. Stir into creamed mixture. Chill at least 1 hour.

On well-floured surface roll ¼ of dough at a time into 8x12-inch rectangle. Cut crosswise in six 2-inch strips. Spread about 2 tablespoons Fig Filling down center of three strips. Moisten edges and top with remaining strips. Press lengthwise edges together with floured fork. Cut in 2-inch lengths. Bake on *ungreased* cookie sheet at 375° about 10 minutes. Makes 4 dozen.

Fig Filling: Combine 2 cups finely chopped dried figs, ½ cup granulated sugar, 1 cup orange juice, and dash salt. Cook, stirring occasionally, till mixture is thick, about 5 minutes. Cool.

Fig Fruit Salad

½ cup dried figs
1 8¾-ounce can crushed pineapple
• • •
1 3-ounce package cream cheese, softened
1 tablespoon mayonnaise or salad dressing
1 tablespoon honey
• • •
2 medium unpared apples, diced
2 medium bananas

Steam figs in a sieve over hot water about 20 minutes; cool. Clip stems; cut figs in thin strips. Drain pineapple, reserving 2 tablespoons syrup. Beat syrup, cheese, mayonnaise, and honey together till smooth. Toss figs, apples, and drained pineapple with dressing. Chill. Before serving, peel and slice bananas; toss with fruit mixture. Serves 6.

FILBERT—A small, thick-shelled nut grown on a bushy shrub or oriental hazel tree. The shell is smooth, medium brown in color, and has a light-colored tip. The nut meat is covered with a thin brown skin which may or may not be removed.

Named for St. Philbert of France, the French people set aside August 22 to recognize him and to gather filberts. The filbert is now used commercially and has been since the early 1900s. Although filberts are also known as hazelnuts, hazelnut refers to a wild nut.

Filberts are imported from Italy, Turkey, and Spain, but are also grown commercially in the northwestern United States. The cultivated varieties are larger and more flavorful than wild hazelnuts.

Available all year round, shelled or unshelled, filberts are sold by the pound. When buying nuts in the shell, be sure the shell is smooth and clean and so well-filled it does not rattle. Store filberts in a cool place away from light.

Filberts can be used in most recipes calling for nuts. They contribute a mild, sweet flavor. The nuts can be ground, sliced, or chopped satisfactorily. Blanch the nuts by toasting in a warm oven for 20 minutes or till the skins rub off.

Filberts are excellent flavorings for desserts, coffee cakes, and ice creams. Add chopped filberts to candies and use whole nuts for garnishing desserts. Give texture to salads and main dishes with sliced filberts. (See also *Nut*.)

Filbert Meringues

Fancy shells to bake ahead of the party—

Beat 2 egg whites to soft peaks. Gradually add ½ cup sugar, beating till very stiff peaks form and sugar is dissolved. Fold in ½ cup finely chopped filberts.

Cover baking sheet with plain paper. Draw 6 circles 3½ inches in diameter; spread each with ⅓ cup meringue. Using back of spoon, shape into shells. Bake at 275° for 1 hour. (For crisper meringues, turn off heat; let dry in oven with door closed about 1 hour.)

Fill with coffee ice cream or top with chocolate sauce, if desired. Makes 6 shells.

Filbert Macaroons

> 1 3½-ounce package whole
>   unblanched filberts (about 1 cup)
> 2 egg whites
> 1 teaspoon lemon juice
> 1 cup sifted confectioners' sugar
> ¼ teaspoon ground cinnamon
>   Whole filberts (optional)

Grind filberts, using coarse blade of food grinder. Beat egg whites with lemon juice till stiff peaks form. Carefully fold in confectioners' sugar, ground nuts, and cinnamon. Drop macaroons onto greased cookie sheet, using 2 teaspoons mixture for each. Top each with nut. Bake at 350° for 15 to 20 minutes. Makes 24.

Filbert Sponge Cake

Coffee powder provides a flavor bonus—

> 1 cup unblanched filberts
> 1 tablespoon instant coffee powder
> 6 egg yolks
> 1 teaspoon vanilla
> 1½ cups sifted cake flour
> 2 teaspoons baking powder
> ¾ cup sugar
> 6 egg whites
> ½ teaspoon salt
> ¾ cup sugar

Grind filberts, using fine blade. Dissolve coffee powder in ½ cup water. Beat egg yolks till thick and lemon-colored. Add coffee and vanilla; beat well. Sift cake flour, baking powder, and ¾ cup sugar together two times. Add to yolk mixture; mix smooth. Stir in nuts.

Wash beaters. Beat egg whites with salt till soft peaks form. Gradually add ¾ cup sugar, beating till stiff peaks form. Fold batter into egg whites, ⅓ at a time. Turn into *ungreased* 10-inch tube pan and bake at 325° for 60 to 65 minutes. Invert to cool.

Elegant nut cake

Sprinkle with confectioners' sugar and perch → whole filberts atop Filbert Sponge Cake. Slice thin and serve with coffee.

Filbert Ice Cream Cake

    1 pint vanilla ice cream
    1 cup snipped dates
    1 cup boiling water
    1 cup butter or margarine
    1 cup sugar
    2 eggs
    ½ teaspoon orange extract
    1¾ cups sifted all-purpose flour
    ¼ cup unsweetened cocoa powder
    1 teaspoon baking soda
    ½ teaspoon salt
    3 ounces chopped filberts,
        toasted (¾ cup)
    2 squares semisweet chocolate,
        grated or shaved (2 ounces)

Stir ice cream to soften; spread evenly in foil-lined 8x1½-inch layer cake pan. Freeze firm. Combine dates and boiling water; cool. Cream butter or margarine and sugar till light and fluffy; beat in eggs and orange extract. Sift together flour, cocoa powder, soda, and salt; add to creamed mixture alternately with date mixture, beating after each addition. Turn into two greased and lightly floured 8x1½-inch layer cake pans. Sprinkle toasted filberts over batter. Bake at 350° till cake tests done, about 30 to 35 minutes. Cool layers thoroughly, nut side up, on racks; sprinkle with grated chocolate, and chill. Place one cake layer on serving plate; add ice cream layer and top with second cake layer. Serve immediately.

FILÉ (*fuh lā', fē lā'*)—Powdered sassafras leaves used as a thickening and flavoring agent particularly in gumbo and other creole dishes which gives the texture of okra. Choctaw Indian squaws taught New Orleans creole cooks that the powdered leaf should be added to the dish after it has been removed from the heat or it will become stringy. (See also *Creole Cookery*.)

FILET MIGNON (*fi lā' min yon', min' yon*)— A small, boneless steak taken from the beef tenderloin. The boneless, tender, and usually expensive beef cut is generally broiled with bacon wrapped around the outside edges. For optimum flavor the filet mignon should be cooked to the rare stage of doneness. (See also *Beef*.)

Filet Mignon Princess

Accompanied by butter-fried potatoes—

In skillet cook 1 tablespoon finely chopped onion in 1 tablespoon butter till tender, but not brown. Mince 2 cups fresh mushrooms; add to onions; cook till liquid is almost gone. Add 2 tablespoons lemon juice and ½ cup red Burgundy wine; reduce to half. Remove from heat. Slightly beat 1 egg yolk; add small amount hot mixture to egg yolk; return to hot mixture; cook and stir till thickened. Fill 4 artichoke cups* with mushroom mixture; keep hot. In another skillet, melt 1 tablespoon shortening; season four 8-ounce center-cut filet mignons with salt and pepper; panbroil 20 minutes, or to desired doneness. Remove from heat; place on stuffed artichoke cups. Pour excess fat from skillet; add ½ cup red Burgundy wine to pan; reduce to half; pour over meat. Place 3 cooked asparagus tips on each steak; top each with 1 tablespoon Béarnaise. Serve with hot panfried potato strips. Serves 4.

Béarnaise Sauce: In small saucepan, combine 3 tablespoons tarragon vinegar, 1 teaspoon minced shallots, 4 crushed peppercorns, and a bouquet of a few tarragon and chervil leaves; simmer till liquid is reduced to half. Strain; add 1 tablespoon cold water to herb liquid. Beat 4 egg yolks in top of double boiler (not over heat); slowly add herb liquid. Have ½ cup butter at room temperature. Add a *few tablespoons* of the butter to egg yolks; place over *hot, not boiling,* water. Cook and stir till butter melts and sauce starts to thicken. Continue adding butter and stirring till all has been used and sauce is smooth as thick cream. Remove from heat at once. Salt to taste and add 1 teaspoon minced fresh tarragon leaves. (Or, add ¼ teaspoon dried whole tarragon leaves and strain sauce.) Makes about 1 cup sauce.

*Available in cans. (These are artichoke bottoms, or *fonds,* 2 inches in diameter.)

FILLED COOKIE—Name given to cookies of rolled, chilled dough cut and filled with jam or sweet mixture. The cookies are filled before baking by sealing the filling between two dough rounds or pulling two ends of a square together over the filling. The baked cookie should have a delicate brown color. (See also *Cookie*.)

Enjoy traditional filet mignon dinner by serving elegant Filet Mignon Princess. Béarnaise Sauce flows atop tower of artichokes, mushroom purée, asparagus tips, and filet mignon.

Date-Filled Sugar Cookies

    1 cup shortening
    ½ cup granulated sugar
    ½ cup brown sugar
    1 egg
    3 tablespoons milk
    1 teaspoon vanilla
    3 cups sifted all-purpose flour
    ½ teaspoon baking soda
    Date Filling

Cream shortening and sugars till fluffy. Add egg, milk, and vanilla; beat well. Sift together dry ingredients and ½ teaspoon salt; add to creamed mixture; mix well. Chill dough 1 hour. On floured surface roll *half* dough at a time to less than ⅛ inch. Cut with 2½-inch round cutter. With tiny cutter or thimble, cut small hole in center of half the cookies. Place scant tablespoon Date Filling on each plain cookie. Top with cutout cookie; press edges with inverted teaspoon tip to seal. Bake 1 inch apart, on *ungreased* cookie sheet at 350° for 10 to 12 minutes. Makes 2½ dozen.

Date Filling: Combine 2 cups snipped dates, ⅓ cup sugar, and ½ cup water. Bring to boiling; cover and simmer about 5 minutes, stirring occasionally. Add 2 tablespoons lemon juice and ¼ teaspoon salt. Cool filling before placing atop cookie dough circles.

Use your fingers to pinch two opposite corners of rolled cookie dough squares together to encase jam or filling in filled cookie.

FILLED MILK — Fresh milk from which natural milk fat has been removed and replaced with another fat, usually coconut oil. The milk used is either nonfat dry milk reconstituted with water, or fluid skim milk. The latter product sometimes contains extra milk solids. Filled milks are subject to numerous state regulations; nutritionally, they may or may not be similar to whole milk. In any event, the use of coconut oil does not reduce the cholesterol value of filled milk. (See also *Milk*.)

FILLET (*fil′ it*) — 1. Boned flesh or meat removed from fish, poultry, or game. 2. The process of removing meat from bones of fish, poultry, or game. The word is often confused with filet which refers to the French delicacy, filet mignon.

A large fish can be filleted successfully by cutting down the middle of the back (starting at tail end) carefully slicing flesh away from the center bone section just to the head. This flat slice often makes an individual serving.

The fillet of beef refers to the tenderloin cut or a portion of the sirloin. The fleshy part of the thigh becomes the fillet of veal and mutton. Poultry and winged game fillets come from the underside or the breast of the animal.

FILLING — A sweet or nonsweet food mixture used in sandwiches, pastry shells, and desserts. Filling often refers to a stuffing for meat or poultry, too. The filling not only adds flavor to the food but also provides contrast in texture and color.

Some fillings are smooth, such as frosting or whipped cream between cake layers. Other fillings contain meat, egg, or cheese and are used to make sandwiches.

Types and kinds: Fillings can fall into one of two categories—sweet or nonsweet. The ingredients used to make the filling determine the category.

1. Nonsweet fillings are used for sandwiches and for nonsweet pastry shells, such as those that are used for some hors d'oeuvres and meat-vegetable pies. The fillings include foods such as meats, fish, cheese, and eggs along with olives, pickles, relishes, and vegetables.

When making nonsweet sandwich fillings, be sure the mixture is soft enough to spread without tearing the bread. Also spread softened butter or margarine, as well as salad dressing or mayonnaise, over the bread before adding the filling.

The filling is prepared with crisp vegetables and mayonnaise or salad dressing just before serving: cream butter before mixing with fish, meats, or vegetables for butter fillings. When making rolled sandwiches, choose a moist filling that helps hold the sandwich together. A tiny appetizer sandwich should be savory and appealing. Select a colorful garnish that is appropriate to the filling.

Tuna Rounds

    1 6½- or 7-ounce can tuna, drained
    ½ cup mayonnaise or salad dressing
    1 5-ounce can water chestnuts,
          drained and chopped
    1 tablespoon minced onion
    1 teaspoon lemon juice
    1 teaspoon soy sauce
    ½ teaspoon curry powder
       Party rye bread

Combine ingredients and mix thoroughly. Spread tuna mixture on slices of small rounds of rye bread. Trim each open-face sandwich with a pimiento-stuffed green olive slice, if desired. Makes about 36 open-face tea sandwiches.

Most sandwich fillings may be stored in the refrigerator in a covered container. Avoid storing cream cheese fillings as they turn yellow and dry out with storage. Sandwiches to be frozen should be spread with butter instead of salad dressing before filling so they do not become soaked.

2. The second type of filling, sweet filling, embellishes cakes, pies, and other desserts to make them deliciously rich. Ingredients used for sweet fillings include fruits, nuts, dates, raisins, mincemeat, and coconut, along with whipped cream, honey, and buttery syrups.

Cake fillings are often the frosting used between the layers, or they may be a specially prepared filling such as a fruit or a cream filling. To fill a layer cake, make sure all the layers are approximately the same thickness. Slice off any humps after baking to make the layers uniform in thickness. Brush crumbs from the cake and lay the first layer bottom side up. (This makes the cake stand straighter.) With spatula, spread about one cup of the filling to the edges. (Spread to within one inch of edge if the filling is very soft.)

The cake filling should be at least 3/16 inch thick for flavorful eating. Spread filling quickly and position second layer with top side up. If the cake has more than two layers, position all layers except the top one with bottom sides up. Place the top layer with the top side up. Allow filling to firm a few minutes before frosting the outside of the cake.

Elegant torte desserts layered with pro-portioned amounts of cake, filling, and fruit are an excellent party or family treat. Some traditional torte recipes re-quire many hours of preparation, while others use quick and easy shortcuts.

Della Robbia Torte

Prepare 1 package lemon chiffon cake mix ac-cording to package directions. Grease the *bottoms only* of three 9x1½-inch round pans. Di-vide batter among pans and bake at 350°, 30 to 35 minutes. Invert to cool. If desired, brush tops of cake layers with rum, using ½ cup white rum; let layers stand 20 minutes.

Prepare one 3- or 3¼-ounce package *regular* vanilla pudding mix according to package di-rections *but use only 1½ cups milk*. Add 1 tea-spoon vanilla. Cover mixture; chill in the re-frigerator, stirring once or twice. Beat smooth; fold in 1 cup whipping cream, whipped.

Spread pudding between layers. To make glaze, melt ½ cup apple jelly; stir in 1 table-spoon lemon juice; cool. Arrange one 8½-ounce can pineapple slices, drained and halved; 5 drained, canned pear halves; 5 drained, canned apricot halves; and 11 maraschino cherries over the top of the cake. Position the pineapple slices around outer edge with pears in center and cherries dropped atop. Spoon cooled glaze over fruit. Chill 5 to 6 hours.

Easy-to-prepare Della Robbia Torte uses packaged lemon cake mix, vanilla pudding mix, and canned fruits to create a rich dessert that looks as though it took hours to make.

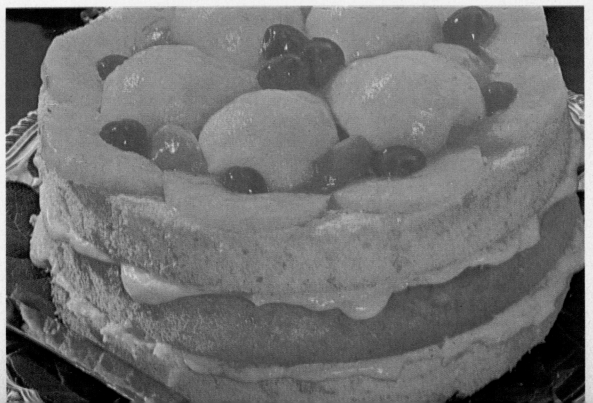

Jelly cake rolls lend themselves to delicious filling recipes. Jam or jelly fillings may be used when the dessert is served at room temperature. Chill the jelly roll before cutting when serving it with a filling of either whipped cream or pudding.

Walnut Cream Roll

Beat 4 egg yolks till thick and lemon-colored. Combine 4 egg whites, 1 teaspoon vanilla, and ½ teaspoon salt. Beat till soft peaks form; gradually add ½ cup sugar, beating till stiff peaks form. Fold egg yolks into whites; carefully fold in ¼ cup sifted all-purpose flour and ½ cup finely chopped walnuts. Spread batter evenly in greased and floured 15½x10½x1-inch jelly roll pan. Bake at 375° till done, about 12 minutes. Test for doneness with pick.

Immediately loosen the sides and turn out on towel sprinkled with confectioners' sugar. Starting at narrow end, roll cake and towel together; cool on rack. Unroll; spread with 1 cup whipping cream, sweetened and whipped. Roll cake; chill before serving.

Cookie fillings are most often sandwiched between two rolled dough cookie rounds. The edges are carefully pinched together to seal the filling so that it does not escape during baking. Delicious date and raisin fillings with nuts are popular for tasty filled cookies and cakes.

Date–Nut Filling

Combine 1½ cups pitted dates, cut up; 1 cup water; ⅓ cup sugar; and ½ teaspoon salt in saucepan; bring to boiling. Cook and stir over low heat till thick, about 4 minutes. Remove from heat; cool. Fold in ½ cup chopped walnuts. Makes about 1½ cups. *Note:* If cake is being topped with Seven-Minute Frosting (See *Frosting*), reserve ¼ cup of the frosting and fold in filling mixture.

Mouth-watering pie fillings of fruit, custard, chiffon, pumpkin, and others in a delicate, flaky pastry are sure signs of an excellent cook. There are as many types of fillings as there are favorite kinds of pies. Rich, creamy fillings are soft and smooth, yet firm enough to hold their shape.

Cream Filling

Use plain or flavored variations—

⅓ cup granulated sugar
3 tablespoons all-purpose flour
¼ teaspoon salt
1¼ cups milk
1 beaten egg
1 tablespoon butter or margarine
1 teaspoon vanilla

In saucepan combine sugar, all-purpose flour, and salt. Gradually add milk; mix well. Cook and stir over medium heat till mixture thickens and bubbles; cook and stir 2 minutes longer. Very gradually stir in the hot flour mixture into the beaten egg; return to saucepan. Cook and stir till mixture just boils. Stir in butter and vanilla; cover surface of filling with waxed paper or clear plastic wrap. Cool. (Don't stir during cooling.) Makes 1½ cups.

Butterscotch Filling: Prepare Cream Filling, *substituting* ⅓ cup brown sugar for ⅓ cup granulated sugar. *Increase* butter from 1 tablespoon to 2 tablespoons.

Chocolate Filling: Prepare Cream Filling, increasing granulated sugar from ⅓ cup to ½ cup. Cut up one 1-ounce square unsweetened chocolate. Add with milk.

Sometimes fillings for individual deep-dish pies are prepared separately from the crust. The crust can be baked on a cookie sheet or baking dish and put over the pie filling just before serving.

Flavorful fruit pies can be prepared with canned or fresh fruits from the market. The filling is often thickened with cornstarch, flour, or egg. Eggs also contribute added flavor and richness to the pie.

Many fillings are put in a baked pastry shell and chilled, such as chiffon pies based on gelatin, egg whites, and cooked custard. Frozen ice cream pies are chilled in the freezer. Creamy, jellied fillings use no egg whites and are put into a baked pastry and chilled.

Lemon Filling

Pour creamy fruit filling in baked, flaky pastry—

¾ **cup sugar**
2 **tablespoons cornstarch**
  Dash salt
¾ **cup cold water**
2 **slightly beaten egg yolks**
1 **teaspoon grated lemon peel**
3 **tablespoons lemon juice**

. . .

1 **tablespoon butter or margarine**

In saucepan combine sugar, cornstarch, and salt; gradually add cold water. Stir in beaten egg yolks, grated lemon peel, and lemon juice. Cook and stir over medium heat till thickened and bubbly. Boil 1 minute; remove from heat. Stir in butter or margarine. Cool to room temperature without stirring. Makes 1⅓ cups.

Lime Filling: Prepare Lemon Filling *substituting* 1 teaspoon grated lime peel and 3 tablespoons lime juice for lemon peel and lemon juice. Add drop green food coloring and butter.

Orange Filling: Prepare Lemon Filling, *substituting* ¾ cup orange juice for the ¾ cup water and the 3 tablespoons lemon juice. Omit 1 teaspoon grated lemon peel.

Delicious breads and coffeecakes warm from the oven with rich, spicy fruit and nut fillings are a welcome sight to anyone. Fill rich dough with nutmeats, candied fruits, fruit peels, and spices.

Jeweled Banana Bread

⅔ **cup sugar**
⅓ **cup shortening**
2 **eggs**
1¾ **cups sifted all-purpose flour**
2¾ **teaspoons baking powder**
1 **cup mashed banana (2 large)**

. . .

¾ **cup mixed candied fruits and peels**
½ **cup chopped walnuts**
¼ **cup raisins**

In a bowl cream sugar and shortening till light. Add eggs, one at a time, beating well. Sift together flour, baking powder, and ½ teaspoon salt; add to creamed mixture alternately with banana. Fold in the remaining ingredients. Pour into a greased 8½x4½x2⅝-inch loaf pan. Bake at 350° till done, about 60 to 70 minutes. Cool bread in pan 20 minutes.

Spread walnut-flavored cake roll with sweet whipped cream and roll to make Walnut Cream Roll dessert for the coffee crowd. Top with whipped cream and crunchy walnut halves.

Pineapple Crisscross Coffee Cake

        2 packages active dry yeast
    4½ to 4¾ cups sifted all-purpose
            flour
    1¼ cups milk
    ½ cup sugar
    ¼ cup shortening
        2 eggs
        1 teaspoon grated lemon peel
        3 tablespoons butter or margarine
            melted
            Pineapple-Coconut Filling

In a large mixer bowl combine yeast and 2½ *cups* of the flour. Heat together the milk, sugar, shortening, and 2 teaspoons salt just till warm, stirring occasionally to melt shortening. Add to dry mixture in mixing bowl; add eggs and lemon peel. Beat at a low speed with electric mixer for ½ minute, scraping sides of bowl constantly. Beat for 3 minutes at high speed. By hand, stir in enough of remaining flour to make a soft dough. Turn out on a lightly floured surface. Knead till smooth and satiny, about 8 minutes. Place in a greased bowl, turning once to grease surface. Cover and let rise till double, about 1¾ hours.

Punch down and divide dough into 3 portions; cover and let rest 10 minutes. Roll each portion into 12x8-inch rectangle and place on greased baking sheet. Brush dough with melted butter and spread Pineapple-Coconut Filling lengthwise down center third of dough. With scissors, make cuts 2 inches in from the side at 1-inch intervals along edges of dough. Alternately fold strips over filling in herringbone fashion. Cover and let rise till double, 45 minutes. Brush top with slightly beaten egg white and sprinkle with ½ cup toasted almonds, if desired. Bake at 350° for 25 to 30 minutes.

Pineapple-Coconut Filling: Combine one 20-ounce can crushed pineapple, well drained; one 3½-ounce can shredded coconut, toasted; ½ cup brown sugar; and ¼ teaspoon cinnamon.

Bake bread in the morning

←— Bake Apricot Bubble Balls, Double-Decker Coffee Strips, Cranberry Wagon-Wheel Rolls, Pineapple Crisscross or Cherry Lattice Coffee Cake for a special brunch.

Double-Decker Coffee Strips

Rich dough contains a rich prune filling—

Soften 1 package active dry yeast in ¼ cup warm water. Cool ⅓ cup scalded milk to lukewarm; stir into yeast mixture; set aside.

Combine 2 cups sifted all-purpose flour, ¼ cup sugar, 1 teaspoon grated lemon peel, and ½ teaspoon salt. Cut in ¼ cup shortening till it resembles coarse cornmeal. Add the yeast-milk mixture and 1 beaten egg; mix. Place in a greased bowl, turning to grease surface. Cover and let rise till double (1¼ to 1½ hours).

Punch down and turn out on floured surface. Roll to 12x10-inch rectangle; place on greased baking sheet. Combine 1 cup chopped, cooked prunes, 3 tablespoons sugar, 1 teaspoon lemon juice, and ⅛ teaspoon ground cinnamon. Spread prune mixture lengthwise over half the dough; fold remaining dough over filling and seal. Cover; let rise till double, about 45 minutes. Bake at 350° for 15 minutes. Cool; frost with confectioners' icing, if desired.

Apricot Bubble Balls

Filling is dropped between rich dough balls—

In a large mixer bowl combine 2 packages active dry yeast and 1½ cups sifted all-purpose flour. Heat together ¾ cup milk, ⅓ cup sugar, ⅓ cup shortening, and 1 teaspoon salt just till warm, stirring to melt shortening. Add to the dry mixture in a mixing bowl; add 2 eggs. Beat at low speed with electric mixer for ½ minute, scraping sides of bowl. Beat 3 minutes at high speed. By hand, stir in 1½ to 2 cups sifted all-purpose flour to make soft dough. Place in greased bowl, turning to grease surface. Cover; let rise till double (2 hours).

Punch down; divide dough into 3 portions. Cover; let rest 10 minutes. Divide portions into 9 pieces; shape into balls. Roll balls in ¼ cup melted butter or margarine; then in mixture of ½ cup sugar and 1 teaspoon ground cinnamon.

Arrange in layers in greased 10-inch tube pan, staggering balls; drop ⅔ cup apricot preserves from teaspoon between balls and sprinkle with nuts. Cover; let rise till double, about 45 minutes. Bake at 350° till done, about 35 to 40 minutes. Cool 10 minutes in pan. Invert and remove from pan.

Cranberry Wagon Wheel Rolls

      2 packages active dry yeast
   4¾ to 5¼ cups sifted-all-purpose
         flour
   1⅓ cups milk
    ½ cup sugar
    ½ cup shortening
   1¼ teaspoons salt
      2 eggs
        Cranberry-Apple Filling

In a large mixer bowl, combine yeast and 2½ cups of the flour. Heat together the milk, sugar, shortening, and salt just till warm, stirring occasionally to melt shortening. Add to dry mixture in mixing bowl; add eggs. Beat at low speed with electric mixer for ½ minute, scraping sides of bowl constantly. Beat 3 minutes at high speed. By hand, stir in enough of the remaining flour to make a soft dough. Turn out on lightly floured surface; knead till smooth and satiny, about 8 to 10 minutes. Place dough in greased bowl, turning once to grease surface. Cover and let dough rise till double, about 1½ hours.

Punch down; divide and form into 2 balls. Let rest 10 minutes. Divide each ball into about 8 pieces and form each of these into a bun. Place the buns about 2 inches apart on a greased baking sheet; flatten slightly. Cover and let rise till double. Make an indentation in each bun, leaving ½-inch edge around roll. Fill in with Cranberry-Apple Filling. Bake at 400° till done, about 15 minutes. Remove from baking sheet immediately and sprinkle rolls with sifted confectioners' sugar, if desired.

Cranberry-Apple Filling: In blender container at low speed chop 1½ cups cranberries and 2 small apples. Add ¾ cup sugar and 1½ teaspoons ground cinnamon; blend.

Cherry Lattice Coffee Cake

      1 package active dry yeast
    ¼ cup warm water
    ⅔ cup butter
    ⅓ cup sugar
      1 teaspoon salt
      4 beaten eggs
      4 cups sifted all-purpose flour
    ¾ cup milk
        Cherry Filling
    ¼ cup sifted all-purpose flour

Soften the yeast in warm water. Cream together butter, ⅓ cup sugar, and salt. Reserve 1 tablespoon of beaten eggs for use later and add remaining eggs to creamed mixture; beat well. Stir in the flour alternately with the softened yeast and the milk. Mix, but do not beat.

Set aside 1 cup of dough and spread remainder in 2 well-greased 9x9x2-inch baking pans. Cover with Cherry Filling.

For lattice, blend ¼ cup sifted all-purpose flour into reserved dough. Divide into 12 parts; roll each between floured hands to make 9-inch strips. Arrange 6 strips in lattice pattern over cherry filling in each pan. Brush the strips with reserved beaten egg. Cover; let rise till double, about 45 minutes. Bake at 375° for approximately 20 to 25 minutes.

Cherry Filling: Combine ½ cup each softened butter, chopped almonds, sugar, and cherry preserves. Mix well.

The ultimate goal is to have a filling with a color, flavor, and texture that is compatible with that of the bread or pastry it supplements. Delicious combinations can be achieved by imaginatively pairing up favorite foods and flavors. (See *Cake, Dessert, Pie* for additional information.)

FILO (*fē′ lō*)—Flaky tissue-paper thin sheets of Greek pastry used in making appetizers and desserts, such as *baklava.* Pastry rolls are made of filo with honey and nut fillings. Layers of filo pastry and vegetables, meat, or cheese make interesting luncheon dishes. One-pound packaged rolls of filo sheets can be found in the frozen foods department of supermarkets in Greek neighborhoods.

FINE CHAMPAGNE—A high-quality French brandy made from certain grapes in the Cognac region of France. It is a blend of Grande and Petite Champagne cognacs. The quality of fine champagne outside France may differ a bit from the splendid brandy that is made in France.

FINES HERBES (*fēn′ erbz*)—A French phrase describing a combination of finely chopped herbs used for seasoning. Often, *fines herbes* refers to chopped parsley only. There may be more than two herbs in *fines herbs,* and they may either be chopped or minced. In earlier times, mushrooms and truffles were also added to the *fines herbes* seasoning.

Herbs now used in *fines herbes* include parsley, tarragon, basil, thyme, and chives. If a combination of the seasoning is made at home, it should be stored in a tightly covered container.

This distinct seasoning is used for soups, stews, omelets, salads, steaks, egg dishes, and sauces. (See also *Herb.*)

Pimiento-Onion Relish

- ⅔ cup water
- ⅓ cup cider vinegar
- ½ teaspoon fines herbes
- 2 tablespoons sugar

. . .

- 1 4-ounce can or jar whole pimientos, quartered
- 1 medium onion, thinly sliced

Combine water, cider, vinegar, fines herbes, and sugar. Add pimientos and onion; marinate overnight. Drain; serve with meat.

FINISHING SAUCE—A French method of thickening and adding flavor to a sauce by swirling butter into the cooked sauce right before serving. To mix the butter into the sauce, lift the saucepan and move it in a circular motion. Do not stir the butter into the sauce as this will prevent thickening. This method insures a smooth, creamy sauce, an even blend of ingredients, and gives a French taste to the sauce.

FINNAN HADDIE (*fin' uhn had' ē*)—The name for haddock that has been smoked and has a light, golden color. It is believed to have been named after the Scottish fishing port, Findhorn, where finnan haddie were first made. In England, one often finds finnan haddie on the breakfast menu.

Much of what is eaten in the United States comes from the New England area and is prepared from large haddock fillets. As with other fish, finnan haddie is a source of protein and the B vitamins, thiamine, riboflavin, and niacin. A 2½x2½x ¼-inch piece equals 103 calories. A common way of preparing this smoked fish is by baking it in a cream sauce or milk. The creamed fish is tasty served over hot, toasted bread. Use finnan haddie in fish casseroles and main dishes. Or, dab melted butter over pieces of fish and broil the pieces till done. (See also *Haddock.*)

FINO (*fē' nō*)—A dry, Spanish sherry that is blended with other types of sherry and shipped under various brand names. Rated as the best by sherry lovers, fino of sturdy body and clean bouquet is produced in the Jerez region of Spain. This very pale sherry is best served after it has been chilled. The rich, dry flavor is compatible with soups. Fino is sometimes served as an appetizer when entertaining. (See also *Sherry.*)

FINOCHIO (*fi nō' kē ō*)—A succulent bulbous-based Italian vegetable, related to the fennel family. Italian truck gardeners introduced finochio to the American vegetable growers and markets.

The large bulbous base, fleshy and sweet, is the most imporant, useful part of the plant. The ornamental stalk foliage is not used as much as the plant base. The knobs are bleached pure white for two weeks after the bulbous base knobs have reached the sized of hens' eggs. Bleaching is done by banking soil against the roots to ward off the sun. This causes the roots to become pure white. The thick plant, which grows low, yields about two crops a year. One crop appears on the market in the early summer and the second crop usually by early winter.

Sometimes the finochio stalks, if they are young and tender, are eaten with salt as celery is eaten. The stalks have a pleasant taste with a slight anise flavor. Other times the bulb of the plant is cut into strips like celery hearts and carrots and eaten like celery. Finochio may be sliced and served raw or slightly blanched in a salad dressed with vinegars and oils.

The finochio base is also used for appetizers and main dishes. The solid base may be cut and served as hors d' oeuvres. As a hot vegetable, the base is often steamed or braised and served au gratin style or with cream sauce.

FISH

Add variety to the menu with protein-rich fresh- or saltwater fish.

Fish range in size from less than one inch to many feet in length, and are either full-bellied or flat, and range in color from a shimmering translucent to a glorious panorama of yellows, greens, reds, and blues. Some fish are docile, fin flickering creatures, while others are armed with sword-shaped noses, or have gaping mouths filled with file-sharp teeth.

The dictionary defines a fish as "any of a large group of cold-blooded animals living in water and having backbones, permanent gills for breathing, fins, and, usually scales. " While this is an accurate definition of a fish, it does not even hint of the manner in which fish have been regarded and used throughout history.

Historically, fish have played a vital role as a religious symbol, as a commercial industry, and, of course, as a food.

Despite their sometimes ferocious appearance, fish were not regarded as food by early Britain's and islanders in the Aegean Sea, but as sacrificial objects for the gods. In fact, many of these pagan people did not eat fish and were quite horrified when they observed dead fish washed up onto the shore for fear that this was a sign of their god's displeasure.

Symbolically the fish has served many purposes. At one time it was used as a substitute for money and as a medium of barter. But its greatest use as a symbol was as a sign of recognition for Christians, in the early days of that religion, when their faith was outlawed by the Romans. When two Christians met, one would sketch out a S in the sand and the other would complete the 8 to indicate that he, too, was a member of the faith.

Religion also has played a vital role in establishing the fishing industry. For example, the Roman Catholic church helped bolster the flagging fishing industries in predominantly Catholic countries by banning meat on Fridays and on Saint days and allowing only fish to be eaten.

The abundance of fish, a natural food which does not require a time of gestation, was probably one of the reasons why the early pilgrims settled near the ocean when they fled from Europe to practice their own religious beliefs in the American colonies. Because of the availability of fish the pilgrims did not have to wait for the season when the crops they had sown ripened and were harvested.

As the pioneers moved inland through the St. Lawrence Valley and up the Mississippi River, they copied the fishing techniques of the Indians and made fish a staple of their diet. And, as they moved across the continent, they established small fish industries—especially on the edge of the Great Lakes.

These fish industries later became vital to the nation's economy. On the East Coast, the New England colonies concentrated on saltwater fishing, while in the hinterland, freshwater fishing prevailed to the extent that in the Great Lakes, by 1865, millions of pounds of fish were being caught and processed each year.

Because of the large volume of fishing done each year, the Bureau of Fisheries was established in 1871 to control grading and to certify the quality of the fish.

Nutritional value: Fish products are rich in protein, contain minerals and vitamins, have a varying amount of fat content, and generally are low in calories.

Fish is an excellent source of protein which is used by the body to build and to repair body tissues. This makes fish particularly good for children, the aged, and those recovering from illness when a large amount of protein is necessary. In fact, a four-ounce serving provides about half the amount of protein needed each day.

In addition to being a source of protein, fish is low in connective tissue—good to keep in mind for those on low-bulk diets.

Fish is also a source of the minerals that are needed for proper functioning of the body. Just a few of the minerals include phosphorus, iron, and potassium. The saltwater varieties of fish contain iodine, which is helpful in the prevention of goiter. Two of the minerals, sodium and chlorine, are not found in great amounts in either freshwater or saltwater fish. This makes fish good for low-sodium diets.

Fishery products also contain vitamins. Some of the fat fish, in particular, are especially good sources of vitamin D. The fish liver oils are good sources of the fat soluble vitamins, especially vitamins A and D. All fish, however, contain at least some of the B vitamins.

The fat content varies with the kind of fish (see chart, page 900). Fish oils contain many polyunsaturated fatty acids, which in some instances, can contribute to the reduction of the blood cholesterol level. The term, fat fish, is not necessarily an indication of the size or shape of the fish, but a guide to the fat content: fat fish contain more than five percent fat; lean fish less than five percent.

What fisherman wouldn't be pleased to have his catch turned into a gourmet entrée? Top the Trout Amandine with a butter sauce and serve the Broiled Lake Trout with Pickle Sauce.

Fat and calorie content of fish

Knowing whether the fish is fat or lean and the calorie count aids in diet planning and in selecting the correct cooking method. (The calorie count is for an uncooked 3½-ounce portion or the serving listed.)

Freshwater Fish	Fat	Lean	Calories
Carp		*	115
Catfish		*	103
Crappie		*	79
Lake Herring		*	96
Lake Trout	*		241
Pickerel		*	84
Rainbow Trout		*	195
Walleye Pike		*	93
Whitefish (1 piece 3x3x⅞″)	*		155
Yellow Perch (1 medium)		*	91

Saltwater Fish

	Fat	Lean	Calories
Butterfish	*		169
Cod (1 piece 3x3x¾″)		*	78
Croaker		*	96
Eel (1 serving)	*		233
Flounder (1 piece 3x3x⅜″)		*	68
Grouper		*	87
Haddock (1 fillet)		*	79
Hake		*	74
Halibut (1 piece 3x2x1″)		*	100
Mackerel (Atlantic)	*		191
Mullet		*	146
Pollock		*	95
Pompano (1 piece 3x3x¾″)	*		166
Red Snapper		*	93
Rockfish		*	97
Salmon (Chinook)	*		222
Sea Bass		*	96
Sole (1 piece 3x3x⅜″)		*	68
Swordfish (1 piece 3x3x¾″)		*	118
Tuna (fresh)	*		145
Whiting		*	74

For the calorie conscious, you're in for some good news: some fish contain fewer calories than many cuts of beef. Of course, the fat fish will contain a few more calories than lean fish, but both are still good for dieters. If fish is not fried and pouring rich sauces on the fish is avoided, fish is a high-quality protein food especially useful to those counting calories.

Types of fish

With the great number of fish available—over 240 species of finfish and shellfish—the finfish can best be divided into saltwater and freshwater varieties. (Although shellfish are sometimes classified under the category of fish, they differ from finfish because they have a shell and no fins.) (See *Shellfish* for further discussion.)

Finfish can also be divided into two other groups: dermersal, or those that live near the bottom of the water—for example cod, flounder, and sole; and pelagic fish, or those that swim in mid water—for example salmon and mackerel.

There is a difference in flavor between freshwater and saltwater fish and between lake fish and stream fish. This is probably due to various reasons including the feeding habits, which definitely affect flavor.

Sportsmen and commercial fishermen find the Great Lakes and Mississippi Valley especially good sources of freshwater fish. Some of the freshwater varieties include the buffalofish, carp, catfish, chub, lake herring, trout, and whitefish.

Saltwater fish are found in the seas, gulfs, and oceans around the world. In America off the New England coast, however, one can find cod, cusk, eel, flounder of various types, haddock, hake, halibut, Atlantic herring, mackerel, ocean perch, pollock, Atlantic salmon, scup, sea bass, shad, skate, some varieties of smelt, swordfish, tuna, and whiting.

The saltwater fish that are caught in the middle Atlantic coastal area are bluefish, butterfish, cod, croaker, black drum, eel, some kinds of flounder, red and white hake, Atlantic herring, king whiting, mackerel, scup, sea bass, sea trout, shad, skate, spot, striped bass, swellfish, swordfish, tilefish, tuna, and whiting.

In the south Atlantic area from North Carolina down to the east coast of Florida, you can find bluefish, butterfish, croaker, drum, eel, king mackerel, mullet, scup, sea bass, sea trout, shad, sheepshead, Spanish mackerel, and striped bass.

The Gulf of Mexico is another source of saltwater fish, for example, the bluefish, red and black drum, king mackerel, king whiting, mullet, pompano, sheepshead, red snapper, and Spanish mackerel.

On the Pacific coast look for barracuda, cod, halibut, Pacific herring, lingcod, mackerel, rockfish, sablefish, salmon, seabass, shad, Pacific sole, smelt, swordfish, and tuna including the albacore.

Selection of fish

If you are not fortunate enough to have a fisherman in the family, you need not despair of eating fish. You can purchase most types of fish, fresh, frozen, or canned. With the development and improvements over the years of the freezing process, people living almost everywhere are able to enjoy fish all year round.

Fresh fish buying tips: Fresh fish can be purchased in several forms. When buying steaks, fillets, or chunks, choose those cuts that are firm and have a fresh look without a dried-out appearance around the edges. If wrapped, they should be packaged in a moisture-vaporproof material.

When buying a whole or dressed fish or cooking a freshly caught fish, one desirable characteristic to look for is bright, clear, bulging eyes. As the fish becomes stale, the eyes get cloudy and tend to sink. Also, the scales lose their luster and the skin slackens. The flesh, however, should be elastic, yet firm. Avoid fish that has a bad odor as it is probably spoiled.

Market Forms Of Fish

Whole or round: The fish just as it is caught. It has to be scaled and eviscerated (internal organs removed) before cooking. The head, tail, and fins may also be removed.

Drawn: Fish that has been cleaned.

Dressed or **pan-dressed:** Fish that has been cleaned and scaled and usually has had its head, tail, and fins removed. The larger, dressed fish may be cut into steaks or fillets. The term pan-dressed refers to the smaller-sized fish.

Steaks: A cross-section slice from a large, dressed fish. It is usually cut $\frac{5}{8}$ to 1 inch thick. The only bone in the steak is a cross-section of the backbone.

Fillets: Pieces of fish that are cut lengthwise from the sides of the fish away from the backbone. This form of fish is almost bone free. When the flesh is cut from only one side of the fish, it is a single fillet. When it is cut from both sides of the same fish and is held together by uncut meat and skin from the underside of the fish, it is called a butterfly fillet.

Chunks: Cross-section pieces cut from a large, dressed fish. Usually the only bone is a cross section of the backbone.

Portions: Pieces that are larger than sticks, cut from blocks of frozen fish. They can be purchased either as uncooked or partially cooked frozen pieces having a bread coating.

Sticks: Frozen, uniformly-sized pieces of fish cut from a block. They, too, are coated with a batter, then breaded and partially cooked. They must be heated before serving.

Canned: Several varieties and types of fish are processed in this manner and include tuna, salmon, sardines, mackerel, anchovies, fish cakes, soups, stews, chowders, and other products. Advantages of these products are that they can be stored on the shelf and are ready to use.

Cured: Fish that is prepared by either the dry salt method, such as caviar, herring, and mackerel; or brine salted (pickled), such as anchovies, herring, salmon, whiting, or mackerel. After curing some fish are smoked.

Frozen fish buying tips: Fish can be purchased frozen in the following market forms—whole, dressed, steaks, fillets, chunks, portions, and sticks. Look for packages of fish that are solidly frozen with no signs of freezer burn or discoloration. They should have no odor and should be packaged in a moisture-vapor-proof wrap to ensure freshness.

Canned fish buying tips: Anchovies, caviar, cod, haddock, herring, mackerel, and sardines can all be purchased in canned form. However, the two most popular canned fish are tuna and salmon.

Most tuna is packed in vegetable oil or water. However, there is a dietetic pack of tuna that is canned using distilled water and no salt. Tuna is also packed in various-sized pieces—solid pack, chunk-style, grated, and flaked. One can choose either albacore (white) or light tuna.

There are also several canned varieties of salmon from which to choose. The color of the salmon is a good indication of the oil content and the price. The deeper red the color, the higher the oil content, and because of the scarcity and popularity of this fish, the higher the price. Sockeye salmon has the highest oil content and is a deep red color. Pink varieties are lighter in color and have less oil content.

How much fish to buy

The following amounts are for one average main dish serving. When combined with a sauce or served as an appetizer, less will be needed. If diners have hearty appetites, more may be needed.

Whole fish.................12 ounces

Dressed fish.................8 ounces

Fillets, steaks.................5 ounces
   or portions

Fish sticks.................4 ounces

Canned fish.................3 ounces

Storage of fish

Fish is very perishable. In order to maintain the best quality, prepare the fish soon after it is caught or purchased. Fresh fish should be kept iced or refrigerated. If properly wrapped when it is purchased, the fish need not be rewrapped before refrigerating. But to store freshly caught fish, wash under cold water and dry with paper toweling. Wrap tightly in moisture-proof material or place in an airtight container. Be sure to use fresh fish within a day or two after they are caught.

For longer storage, fish should be frozen. Dress and wash the fish, then dip in a salt solution before wrapping and sealing in moisture-vaporproof material. Keep the fish frozen until ready to cook. Do not freeze uncooked, lean fish for longer than six months and fat fish for longer than three months to ensure quality eating.

To store cooked fish, cover tightly and refrigerate not longer than three or four days. Or, if desired, freeze the cooked fish, which has been tightly wrapped, for no longer than three months.

Normally, canned fish should not be stored longer than one year for best quality. Keep it in a cool, dry place.

Preparing fish

The catch of the family's fisherman must be cleaned the same day that it is caught. Have the proper equipment on hand so that cleaning will be easier.

How to clean small fresh fish: After the fish is washed, scrape off the scales with a knife or scraper, working toward the head. Making a ¼-to ½-inch deep cut parallel to the fins, slice along each side of the dorsal fin (large fin on fish's back that is on top of backbone) and anal fin (fin towards the rear, underneath fish). Hold the fish on its back and make a cut right behind the vent on the underneath side. Slip the knife forward under the skin and cut down to the pectoral fins (fins on the sides) on both sides of fish. With the fish laying on its side, make a deep cut on both sides of the fish's body, just behind the pectoral fins.

Break the backbone by pulling the head upward. Tear the head, entrails, pectoral, and pelvic fins (fins towards the front underneath the fish) loose. Remove dorsal and anal fins giving a quick pull forward towards the head so that the root bones will still be attached. Cut off the tail and wash the fish well before cooking.

How to thaw frozen fish: To thaw fish before cooking, place the fish in its original wrappings in the refrigerator. Allow about 24 hours for a 16-ounce package. Or, if time is short, place the fish, sealed in a plastic bag, under cold, running water. This will take about 1 to 2 hours for a 16-ounce package. Once the fish has thawed, use as soon as possible.

Just a few precautions—do not thaw fish sticks or portions before cooking and do not soak unwrapped fish in water.

Cooking fish

Fish is a relatively easy food to prepare, it is versatile, and it cooks rather quickly. It has very tender meat; consequently, correct cooking techniques are very important so that the fish will be served at its best. The flavor of fish is developed and the protein in fish becomes easier to digest as it is cooked. When properly prepared, fish is moist and tender with a very delicate flavor. Because of its versatility, fish is used in many recipes, from appetizers, salads, soups and chowders, to sandwiches and main dishes.

Whether the fish is fat or lean often determines the cooking method. For example, broiling and baking are good methods for cooking fat fish. The fat will keep the fish from drying out during cooking. A lean fish usually is poached, fried, or steamed, but it can be baked or broiled if basted frequently with melted butter or shortening to keep it moist. These are just general guides and almost any fish can be cooked by any method if allowances are made for the fat content of the fish.

The fish is done when the flesh can be easily flaked with a fork and has an opaque appearance. Avoid overhandling the fish during cooking as it is very delicate and tends to flake apart very easily.

Baking: Thaw fish if frozen, and place in a greased, shallow baking pan in a single layer. For fillets, place skin side down and tuck under the thin ends so the fish is an even thickness. A whole fish can be stuffed with a savory mixture before baking. Bake at a moderate oven temperature till fish flakes easily when tested with a fork.

Baked Fish Fillets

    1 pound fresh or frozen fish fillets
    1 tablespoon lemon juice
    ⅛ teaspoon paprika
      Salt and pepper
    1 tablespoon butter or margarine
    1 tablespoon all-purpose flour
    ½ cup milk
    ¼ cup buttered bread crumbs
    1 tablespoon snipped parsley

Thaw frozen fillets; cut into serving-size pieces. Place in greased shallow baking dish. Sprinkle with lemon juice, paprika, salt, and pepper. In saucepan, melt butter or margarine; blend in flour, dash salt, and dash pepper. Add milk; cook and stir till thickened and bubbly. Pour sauce over fillets. Sprinkle with crumbs. Bake at 350° for 35 minutes. Trim with snipped parsley. Makes 3 or 4 servings.

Spinach-Fish Bake

    1 11-ounce package frozen breaded
      fish portions
    1 10-ounce package frozen
      chopped spinach
            • • •
    1 11-ounce can condensed Cheddar
      cheese soup
    2 tablespoons milk
      Dash ground nutmeg
      Lemon wedges

Arrange frozen fish portions in 10x6x1½-inch baking dish. Bake at 425° for 10 minutes. Meanwhile, cook spinach according to package directions; drain thoroughly. Combine with condensed soup, milk, and ground nutmeg. Heat. Spoon over fish in baking dish. Garnish with lemon wedges and return to oven to heat through, about 5 minutes. Serves 4 to 6.

Lemon–Stuffed Fish

½ cup finely chopped celery
¼ cup chopped onion
3 tablespoons butter or margarine
4 cups dry bread cubes
½ teaspoon grated lemon peel
4 teaspoons lemon juice
1 tablespoon snipped parsley
½ teaspoon salt
  Dash pepper
2 16-ounce packages frozen fish
  fillets, partially thawed
1 tablespoon butter or margarine,
  melted
  Paprika

Cook celery and onion in 3 tablespoons butter or margarine till crisp-tender. Pour over bread cubes. Add lemon peel and juice, parsley, salt, and dash pepper; toss together.

Slice each block of partially thawed fish in half horizontally through the center, making 4 thin rectangular pieces. Place 2 pieces in greased 13x9x2-inch baking pan. Spoon *half* the stuffing mixture on each. Top with 1 tablespoon melted butter and sprinkle with salt. Cover pan with foil. Bake at 350° till fish flakes easily with a fork, 20 to 25 minutes. Sprinkle with paprika. Makes 6 servings.

Stuffed Fillet Roll–Ups

Cook 2 tablespoons chopped onion in 2 tablespoons butter till tender. Stir in 2 cups soft bread crumbs, ¼ teaspoon poultry seasoning, ⅛ teaspoon salt, dash pepper, and 2 tablespoons mayonnaise. Partially thaw one 16-ounce package frozen haddock fillets. Cut block of fish in half lengthwise. Then split each piece in half again lengthwise, making 4 strips 8x1½-inches. Completely thaw fish. Spread each piece with bread stuffing; roll up, jelly-roll fashion. Place in 3-cup casserole. Bake, covered, at 375° for 25 minutes. Uncover; bake 10 minutes. Serve with Egg Sauce. Serves 4.

Egg Sauce: Cook 2 tablespoons chopped green onion in 2 tablespoons butter till tender. Blend in 2 tablespoons all-purpose flour, ½ teaspoon salt, and dash pepper. Add 1¼ cups milk, ½ teaspoon prepared mustard, and 1 teaspoon Worcestershire sauce. Cook and stir till bubbly. Add 1 finely chopped hard-cooked egg. Heat.

Herb–Baked Fish

Thaw one 16-ounce package frozen haddock, halibut, *or* cod fillets. Place in 10x6x1½-inch baking dish. Dot the thawed fillets with 1 tablespoon butter or margarine. In saucepan thoroughly blend 1 cup milk and 2 tablespoons all-purpose flour. Cook and stir over medium heat till sauce thickens and bubbles. Cook and stir 1 minute longer. Stir in ¼ teaspoon salt; ¼ teaspoon garlic salt; ⅛ teaspoon pepper; ⅛ teaspoon dried thyme leaves, crushed; dash dried oregano leaves, crushed; and ¼ cup chopped green onion. Mix well.

Pour sauce over fish. Sprinkle lightly with paprika. Bake, uncovered, at 350° till fish tests done, 20 to 25 minutes. Makes 4 servings.

Tuna Italian

½ cup chopped onion
1 tablespoon butter or margarine
1 10½-ounce can condensed cream
  of mushroom soup
1 6-ounce can evaporated milk
⅓ cup grated Parmesan cheese
1 6½- or 7-ounce can tuna, drained
1 3-ounce can sliced mushrooms,
  drained (½ cup)
¼ cup chopped ripe olives
2 tablespoons snipped parsley
2 teaspoons lemon juice
4 ounces noodles, cooked and
  drained (about 2 cups)
  Parmesan cheese
  Paprika

Cook onion in butter till tender but not brown. Add soup, evaporated milk, and cheese; heat and stir. Break tuna in chunks; add with next 5 ingredients. Pour into 2-quart casserole. Sprinkle with additional Parmesan cheese and paprika. Bake at 350° for 25 to 30 minutes. Top with additional snipped parsley and ripe olive slices, if desired. Makes 6 servings.

Tuna and noodle variation

Olives, Parmesan cheese, and lemon juice → are added to make Tuna Italian a specialized version of the family favorite.

Salmon or Tuna Pie

Sure to be a hit with the family—

    2 beaten eggs
    ½ cup milk
    ¼ cup chopped onion
    2 tablespoons snipped parsley
    1 tablespoon butter, melted
    ¾ teaspoon dried basil leaves,
        crushed
    ¼ teaspoon salt
        · · ·
    1 16-ounce can salmon, *or* 2 6½- or
        7-ounce cans tuna, drained
    1 stick piecrust mix
       Creamed peas

Combine eggs, milk, onion, parsley, butter, basil, and salt. Break salmon or tuna into chunks, removing bones and skin from salmon. Add to egg mixture. Pour into well-greased 8-inch pie plate. Prepare piecrust mix according to package directions. Roll ⅛ inch thick; cut circle using bottom of 8-inch pie plate as a guide. Cut the circle into 6 wedges; arrange atop salmon or tuna mixture. Bake at 425° till done, about 25 minutes. Serve at once with creamed peas. Makes 6 servings.

Tuna 'n Rice Soufflé

    1 10½-ounce can condensed cream
        of mushroom soup
    1 6½- or 7-ounce can tuna,
        drained and flaked
    1 cup cooked rice
    ¼ cup chopped canned pimiento
    2 tablespoons snipped parsley
        · · ·
    4 eggs
      Lemon wedges

In saucepan heat and stir soup. Add tuna, rice, pimiento, and parsley; heat through. Remove from heat. Separate eggs. Beat whites till stiff peaks form. Beat yolks till thick and lemon-colored; gradually stir in tuna mixture. Pour slowly onto beaten egg whites, folding together thoroughly. Turn into *ungreased* 2-quart casserole. Bake at 350° till mixture is set in center, 30 to 35 minutes. Serve immediately. Pass lemon wedges. Makes 6 servings.

Remove head and tail. Using table knife, make a gentle lengthwise cut 1 inch from upper edge, cutting in just to backbone.

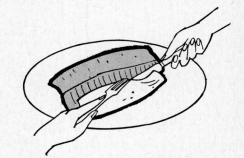

Slide knife along top of backbone gently folding top section away from backbone. Repeat, folding back bottom section.

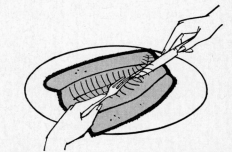

Carefully slide knife under the backbone, lifting it away from body of fish. Use fork to assist. Discard the backbone.

Gently replace the two sections to their original position atop the fish. Head and tail may be replaced, if desired.

Fish in Cheese Sauce

Try this with haddock or halibut—

1 pound fresh or frozen fish steaks
    or fillets, cut in serving-sized
    pieces
1 tablespoon butter or margarine
1/4 teaspoon salt
    Dash pepper
    . . .
1 10-ounce package frozen cut
    asparagus
1 11-ounce can condensed Cheddar
    cheese soup
1/4 cup milk
1 cup soft bread crumbs
2 tablespoons butter, melted

Thaw frozen fish and place in greased 10x6x1½-inch baking dish; dot with 1 tablespoon butter; sprinkle with salt and pepper. Bake at 350° about 30 minutes. Meanwhile, cook asparagus according to package directions; drain. Place asparagus atop fish. Combine soup and milk; pour over all. Combine crumbs and melted butter; sprinkle atop. Return to oven till lightly browned, 10 minutes. Makes 4 servings.

Seafood Turnovers

Dill sauce adds a finishing touch—

1 7¾-ounce can salmon *or*
    1 7-ounce can tuna
1 10½-ounce can condensed cream
    of mushroom soup
1/4 cup chopped celery
    . . .
2 sticks piecrust mix
2 tablespoons milk
    Dash dried dillweed

Drain and flake salmon or tuna, removing bones and skin from salmon. Combine ½ *cup* of the soup, fish, and celery. Prepare piecrust mix according to package directions; roll into four 6-inch circles. Place ¼ of the filling on ½ of each circle; fold to form turnovers. Seal edges with fork; prick top. Bake on *ungreased* cookie sheet at 450° for 15 to 20 minutes. Combine remaining soup, milk, and dillweed; heat. Serve with turnovers. Makes 4 servings.

Planked Stuffed Walleye

1 3-pound dressed walleye *or* pike
    Salt
1/3 cup chopped celery
2 tablespoons chopped onion
1½ teaspoons snipped parsley
2 tablespoons butter
2 cups dry bread cubes
1/2 teaspoon salt
1/2 teaspoon ground sage *or* dried
    marjoram leaves, crushed
    Dash pepper
    Melted butter
4 slices bacon
3 ripe tomatoes, cut in half
    Garlic salad dressing
    Duchess Potatoes
2 10-ounce packages frozen peas,
    cooked and drained

Wash fish; remove head, fins, and backbone, but leave tail on. Rinse again and wipe dry. Rub inside and outside of fish with salt. Let stand 10 minutes.

Cook celery, onion, and parsley in 2 tablespoons butter just till tender. Combine with bread cubes, ½ teaspoon salt, sage, and pepper. Toss lightly. Stuff fish loosely. Skewer; lace.

Place the fish on a seasoned plank or a well-greased bake-and-serve platter. Brush the fish with melted butter. Bake the fish, uncovered, at 375° for 25 minutes. Remove from oven.

Lay bacon strips over fish. Place tomato halves beside the fish and brush the cut surfaces with garlic salad dressing. Pipe Duchess Potatoes around edge of plank. Return to oven and bake till fish flakes, about 15 minutes.

To serve, remove skewers; add peas to remaining space on plank. Makes 6 servings.

Duchess Potatoes: Beat 1 tablespoon butter, 1 beaten egg, and salt and pepper to taste into 4 cups hot mashed potatoes. Using a pastry bag with large star tip, pipe hot potatoes around edge of plank. Drizzle 2 tablespoons melted butter or margarine over potatoes.

Broiling: If fish is frozen, it should be thawed before cooking. Thicker pieces, about one inch, are better for broiling because they will not dry out as fast under the high heat. Place fish on greased broiler pan and baste liberally with melted butter.

Broil about three to four inches from heat till fish flakes easily when tested with fork. Fillets or steaks do not need to be turned over, but whole fish should be turned once, halfway during cooking.

Broiled Lake Trout

**6 1-inch thick lake trout steaks
    (or use northern, young muskie,
    or salmon)
⅓ cup butter or margarine, melted
    Salt and pepper
    Pickle Sauce
    Lemon wedges**

Place fish in a single layer on greased broiler pan. Brush with melted butter or margarine and season with salt and pepper.

Broil about 3 to 4 inches from heat till fish flakes easily when tested with a fork, about 10 to 15 minutes. Brush fish with melted butter once during cooking. Serve with Pickle Sauce lemon wedges. If desired, trim with olive kabobs and parsley sprigs. Makes 6 servings.

Pickle Sauce: Drain ¼ cup chopped dill pickle and 1 tablespoon finely chopped capers on paper toweling. Add to 1 cup mayonnaise or salad dressing. Stir in 1½ teaspoons prepared mustard and 1½ teaspoons snipped parsley.

Herb-Crumb Topped Fish

**2 12-ounce packages frozen
    halibut steaks, thawed
¼ cup butter or margarine, melted
    Salt and pepper
¼ cup dry bread crumbs
⅛ teaspoon dried thyme leaves,
    crushed
    Dash garlic salt**

Place the fish in a single layer on a greased broiler pan. Brush with some of the melted butter or margarine; season with salt and pepper. Broil about 3 to 4 inches from the heat for 8 minutes. Add dry bread crumbs, crushed thyme leaves, and garlic salt to remaining butter or margarine. Sprinkle on fish. Return to the broiler till crumbs are browned and fish flakes easily when tested with a fork, about 3 to 5 minutes longer. Makes 4 to 6 servings.

Fish with Tarragon Butter

Thaw one 16-ounce package frozen fish fillets. Cut fish in 4 serving-sized pieces. Sprinkle fish with salt and pepper. Place on greased broiler pan. Spread with some of the Tarragon Butter. Broil about 3 to 4 inches from the heat till fish flakes easily when tested with a fork, about 10 to 15 minutes. Pass the remaining Tarragon Butter. Makes 4 servings.

Tarragon Butter: Cream ¼ cup softened butter or margarine till fluffy. Then crush ½ teaspoon dried tarragon leaves. Combine tarragon and ½ teaspoon lemon juice with creamed butter. Keep the butter at room temperature for 1 hour to mellow. Refrigerate any leftover butter.

Charcoal broiling: If fish is frozen, it should be thawed before cooking as for oven broiling. Choose thick cuts of fish, since this is a dry heat method of cooking. The pan-dressed fish should be cooked over moderately hot coals about 16 to 20 minutes, while fillets and steaks should be cooked 10 to 16 minutes, turning the fish once during cooking. Use a greased, wire broiler basket so that the fish will be easier to turn.

For a crispy coating on freshly caught trout, dip cleaned fish in a seasoned cornmeal mixture before frying in a skillet.

Charcoaled Salmon Steaks

Brush six 1-inch thick salmon steaks (or use northern, young muskie, or trout) with ⅓ cup melted butter. Place in a greased, wire broiler basket. Broil over *moderately hot* coals for 5 to 8 minutes. Turn, brush with melted butter, and broil till done, 5 to 8 minutes longer. Season with salt and pepper. Combine 1 cup mayonnaise and 1 tablespoon undrained capers. Pass with fish. Makes 6 servings.

Frying: This is a good and popular method of cooking fish. This method adds crispness and it also adds fat to the lean types of fish. The fish may be dipped in an egg or milk mixture, seasoned, then coated with crumbs, cornmeal, or flour before cooking. It can then be panfried, ovenfried, or deep-fat fried. Drain fish after frying to remove any excess fat.

Trout Amandine

Wash 4 pan-dressed brook trout. (*Or* substitute crappies, bluegills, or yellow perch.) Leave tail on but remove head and backbone. Dry. Dip in seasoned all-purpose flour. Melt ¼ cup butter in skillet. Add fish and fry till browned and fish flakes, 12 to 15 minutes, turning once. Remove from pan and keep warm.

Melt an additional ¼ cup butter in skillet, mixing with crusty bits. Add 2 tablespoons slivered almonds. Brown, stirring occasionally. Stir in ¼ cup lemon juice and 2 tablespoons snipped parsley. Season with salt and pepper. Pour over the fish. Makes 4 servings.

Fried Fish

Wash pan-dressed fish; dry thoroughly. Dip in 1 beaten egg mixed with 1 tablespoon water, then in bread crumbs, seasoned flour, or cornmeal. Brown fish in ¼ inch hot shortening on one side. Turn; brown other side.

Oven-Fried Fish

1 pound fresh or frozen fish
    fillets
½ cup milk
½ cup fine dry bread crumbs
2 tablespoons butter, melted

Thaw frozen fillets; cut in serving-sized pieces. Dip in milk; roll in crumbs. Place in greased baking pan. Sprinkle with salt and pepper. Drizzle butter over fish; bake at 500° till fish flakes easily with fork, 10 to 12 minutes. Makes 3 or 4 servings.

Zippy Fish Fillets

2 tablespoons Worcestershire sauce
1 tablespoon lemon juice
1 pound fresh or frozen fish
    fillets
½ cup dry bread crumbs

Combine Worcestershire and lemon juice. Thaw frozen fillets; Cut in serving-sized pieces. Brush with lemon mixture. Season with salt and pepper. Dip in crumbs. Bake in greased baking pan at 500° about 15 minutes. If desired, serve with tartar sauce. Serves 4.

Poaching and steaming: Two moist-heat methods of cooking fish are steaming and poaching. To steam, cook the fish over the steam rising from boiling water. Sometimes the water is seasoned. For steaming fish special equipment is usually required, either a steam cooker or a deep pan with a rack on which the fish is placed.

To poach, cook the fish in a simmering liquid. Again the cooking liquid can be seasoned water, seasoned milk, or a mixture of water and wine, or water and lemon juice. (See also *Shellfish*.)

Poached Fish

If a recipe calls for cooked fish as an ingredient, use this method—

2 to 3 pounds fresh or frozen fish
    fillets or steaks
    Boiling water
1 small onion, quartered
2 teaspoons salt

Thaw frozen fish. Place in greased 10-inch skillet. Add boiling water to cover. Add onion and salt. (Or, substitute Court Bouillon.) Simmer, covered, till fish flakes easily when tested with a fork, 5 to 10 minutes. Carefully remove fish. Use as a main dish with sauce or in recipes using cooked fish. One pound fillets makes 2 cups cooked, flaked fish.

Poached Salmon

Easy to prepare in an electric skillet because temperatures are given in the directions—

4 fresh or frozen salmon steaks, cut
    1 inch thick (1 pound)
1¼ cups dry white wine
2 tablespoons thinly sliced green
    onion with tops
2 or 3 sprigs parsley
1 bay leaf
1 teaspoon salt
    Dash pepper
    • • •
¼ cup whipping cream
2 well-beaten egg yolks
½ teaspoon lemon juice
2 tablespoons snipped parsley

Thaw frozen salmon. In skillet combine wine, onion, parsley sprigs, bay leaf, salt, and pepper. (Electric skillet 350°.) Heat to boiling; add salmon steaks. Cover and reduce heat (220°); simmer till fish flakes easily when tested with fork, about 10 minutes. Remove fish and bay leaf. Keep steaks warm. Discard bay leaf.

Boil wine mixture down to ¾ cup. Combine cream, egg yolks, and lemon juice; slowly add *part* of wine mixture. Return to wine mixture in skillet. Cook and stir over low heat till thickened and bubbly. Spoon over fish. Garnish with snipped parsley. Makes 4 servings.

Steamed Fish

1 pound fresh or frozen fish fillets
    or steaks or 1 3-pound dressed
    fish
2 cups water
1 teaspoon salt

Thaw frozen fish. Bring water to boiling in 10-inch skillet or fish poacher with tight fitting cover. Sprinkle fish with salt. Place fish on a greased rack in pan so that fish does not touch water. Cover pan tightly and steam till fish flakes easily when tested with a fork—fillets, 3 to 4 minutes; steaks, 6 to 8 minutes; dressed, 20 to 25 minutes. Carefully remove fish. Use the fish whole as a main dish with a tart sauce or use flaked in recipes calling for cooked flaked fish as an ingredient.

FISH AND CHIPS—A combination of fried fish fillets and deep-fat fried potatoes. It is a traditional English dish and is often sold wrapped in newspapers.

Fish and Chips

1 pound fresh or frozen fish fillets
1 pound potatoes, peeled
    (3 potatoes)
    Shortening
¼ cup all-purpose flour
½ teaspoon salt
1 egg yolk
2 tablespoons water
1 tablespoon salad oil
1 stiffly beaten egg white
¼ cup all-purpose flour

Thaw frozen fish. Cut into 3 or 4 portions. Cut potatoes into uniform strips, slightly larger than for french fries. Fry potatoes in deep, hot fat (375°) till golden brown, about 7 to 8 minutes. Remove, drain, and keep warm.

Combine ¼ cup flour and salt. Make well in in center, add egg yolk, water, and oil. Stir till batter is smooth. Fold in egg white. Dip fish in ¼ cup flour, then into batter. Fry in deep, hot fat (375°) till golden brown, about 1½ minutes on each side. Sprinkle fish and chips with salt. To serve, sprinkle fish with vinegar, if desired. Makes 3 or 4 servings.